Risk Management and Performance in the Balkans Support Contract

T0162224

Victoria A. Greenfield, Frank Camm

Prepared for the United States Army

Approved for public release; distribution unlimited

 ARROYO CENTER

The research described in this report was sponsored by the United States Army under Contract No. DASW01-01-C-0003.

Library of Congress Cataloging-in-Publication Data

Greenfield, Victoria A., 1964-
    Risk management and performance in the Balkans support contract / Victoria A. Greenfield, Frank Camm.
      p. cm.
    "MG-282."
    Includes bibliographical references.
    ISBN 0-8330-3733-1 (pbk.)
    1. Defense contracts—United States—Case studies. 2. United States. Army—Procurement—Case studies. 3.
    Bosnia and Hercegovina—History, Military—20th century. 4. Bosnia and Hercegovina—History, Military—21st
    century. 5. Operation Allied Force, 1999—Equipment and supplies. I. Camm, Frank A., 1949– II.Title.

    UC267.G754 2005
    355.6'212'0973—dc22

                                                                              2004028146

The RAND Corporation is a nonprofit research organization providing objective analysis and effective solutions that address the challenges facing the public and private sectors around the world. RAND's publications do not necessarily reflect the opinions of its research clients and sponsors.

RAND is a registered trademark.

Published 2005 by the RAND Corporation
1776 Main Street, P.O. Box 2138, Santa Monica, CA 90407-2138
1200 South Hayes Street, Arlington, VA 22202-5050
201 North Craig Street, Suite 202, Pittsburgh, PA 15213-1516
RAND URL: http://www.rand.org/
To order RAND documents or to obtain additional information, contact
Distribution Services: Telephone: (310) 451-7002;
Fax: (310) 451-6915; Email: order@rand.org

Preface

In 2001, the Office of the Assistant Secretary of the Army for Manpower and Reserve Affairs raised a concern that the Army's use of contractors on the battlefield did not stem from any clearly articulated policy and could well be inappropriate. It asked RAND Arroyo Center to identify the policies and processes that appeared to be driving Army decisions to use contractors on the battlefield and offer ways to increase the likelihood that these policies and processes would yield outcomes consistent with the Army's high-level goals.

Arroyo's analysis proceeded along two parallel tracks. One looked from the top down at the risks associated with using contractors on the battlefield and what could be done to manage these risks more effectively. The other examined one of the largest contracts supporting deployed Army forces to understand better how Army use of contractors works from the bottom up. This document details Arroyo's findings from the second track, by applying a risk-management framework to the Balkans Support Contract. The report looks at risk in an ongoing contract. The authors completed most of their analysis in mid-2003, and so the information provided in this document is generally current up to that point. However, in some instances, the authors quote or cite source material predating 2003. In those instances, the names of particular institutions or practices may have changed. Moreover, the authors recognize that since 2003, the contracting environment in other parts of the world has changed dramatically, particularly as it pertains to security. This report should interest those involved in contracting, force structure, or military operations and support planning processes. Arroyo's findings on the first track are reported in Frank Camm and Victoria A. Greenfield, *How Should the Army Use Contractors on the Battlefield? Assessing Comparative Risks in Sourcing Decisions*, MG-296, 2005.

This research was sponsored by the Assistant Secretary of the Army for Manpower and Reserve Affairs and was conducted in RAND Arroyo Center's Manpower and Training Program. RAND Arroyo Center, part of the RAND Corporation, is a federally funded research and development center sponsored by the United States Army.

For more information on RAND Arroyo Center, contact the Director of Operations (telephone 310-393-0411, extension 6419; FAX 310-451-6952; email Marcy_Agmon@rand.org), or visit Arroyo's web site at http://www.rand.org/ard/.

Contents

Figures

Tables and Box

Summary

Contractors provide the Army with services in a wide variety of settings and circumstances, both domestic and international. Recent pressures on the Army to rely more heavily on contractors and the increasingly ill-defined nature of the battlefield raise serious questions for policymakers. Is the Army getting what it needs from its combat service support (CSS) contracts? Do those contracts present any unrecognized, unmitigated, or unnecessary risks? If the Army is not getting what it needs or is accepting inappropriate risks, what can it do about it?

Case studies of CSS contracts can provide some answers. In this report, we present a case study of the Balkans Support Contract (BSC), a CSS contract that has involved deployment. We chose the BSC because of its extensive track record, scope, and size. The contract has provided wide-ranging life support, transportation, and maintenance services to the Army and other end users over several years in a dynamic operating environment. By analyzing the performance of the contract through the lens of risk management, consisting of risk assessment and mitigation, we draw lessons for U.S. policymakers. In so doing, we also compare some of the risks of different sources. We undertake this analysis by examining official records, studies, and press reports and by interviewing customers, contractors, and other observers.

Origins and Key Characteristics

The BSC establishes an opportunity to fill requirements through a designated contractor, but not an obligation. It emerged from two earlier contracts: the Army's Logistics Civil Augmentation Program (LOGCAP) umbrella contract and a derivative sole-source contract.

- In 1992, Brown and Root, now Kellogg Brown and Root (KBR), won the Army's first LOGCAP umbrella contract.
- In 1995, the Army activated the LOGCAP contract in the Balkans.
- In 1997, the Army awarded KBR a sole-source contract in the Balkans.
- In 1999, the Army awarded the BSC to KBR for a five-year term. The contract was awarded through an open competition on the basis of best value.

Given the inherent uncertainties of operating in a contingency environment, the Army has—through the BSC—sought to balance potentially competing demands for preparedness and responsiveness, along with an apparent interest in reducing its in-house role in providing CSS in the region, relating to various resource constraints. For these reasons, the BSC, like the LOGCAP and sole-source contracts, was set up as a preplanned, performance-based, indefinite-delivery, indefinite-quantity (IDIQ) contract, with a cost-plus-award-fee (CPAF) payment structure, devolving responsibility for service coordination and delivery and freeing Army resources, especially manpower, for other core functions.

- In a "preplanned" contract, the contractor develops an implementation plan for a future contingency. The plan typically covers the full range of potential activities posited in the work scope and work breakdown structures.
- A "performance-based" contract generally tells the contractor what the customer wants done but does not tell the contractor how to do it. The BSC lists service requirements in terms of out-

comes. The customer obtains services through task orders, delineated by country.

- An IDIQ contract does not specify the delivery date or exact quantities at the time of the award. This level of generality is desirable when the customer lacks information about timing or quantities.
- A CPAF contract reimburses costs within certain agreed-on limits, typically guarantees a set base fee, and provides performance incentives through award fees, which depend on the contractor's performance. The BSC specifies both fees in terms of the negotiated estimated cost, not the actual cost.

A performance-based, IDIQ, CPAF contract can afford considerable flexibility to the customer and contractor and require less micromanagement than do many other contract types. However, it is not self-governing or without management rights and responsibilities. Indeed, the BSC involves numerous participants, including government contracting and functional personnel drawn from several U.S. Department of Defense (DoD) agencies, various end users, and the contractor and its employees. The U.S. Army Corps of Engineers, Transatlantic Programs Center administers the contract from Winchester, Virginia, and provides the principal contracting officer. The Defense Contract Management Agency contributes field-level administrative contracting officers. Area Support Groups have taken on routine base operations and administrative control functions. The Joint Acquisition Review Board (JARB) is responsible for validating requirements and selecting sources. U.S. Army Europe (USAREUR) funds the contract, and deployed U.S. forces are among the end users. However, only a contracting officer can give direction to the contractor, and only the contractor can give direction to its employees.

The U.S. government is also responsible for providing the BSC contractor and its employees with some support services, including force protection. On a day-to-day basis, the responsibility for protection falls largely to the task force commanders. The Army has tended to limit the contractor's responsibility to passive force protection and to self-defense to better preserve the status of the contractor's employees as "civilians accompanying the force."

Risk Management in Theory and Practice

Army and joint doctrine define risk and provide practical guidance for managing risk. The doctrine tends to be operationally oriented, but the basic framework can be applied to contracting. The doctrine requires systematic consideration of what can go wrong in an operation, including the likelihood and potential severity of the event. Such systematic thinking can facilitate priority-setting for risk control.

Definitions and Practical Guidance

The Army defines *risk* as the "chance of hazard or bad consequences; the probability of exposure to chance of injury or loss from a hazard; risk level is expressed in terms of hazard probability and severity." It further defines *hazard* as "a condition or activity with potential to cause damage, loss, or mission degradation" and any actual or potential condition that can cause injury, illness, or death of personnel; damage to or loss of equipment and property; or mission degradation. Joint doctrine is generally consistent. The 2001 Quadrennial Defense Review Report calls attention to an even wider range of hazards, relating to force management, operations, future challenges, and institutions. Drawing from all three sources, we address potential hazards across wide-ranging military activities and objectives.

Drawing from Army and joint doctrine, Figure S.1 outlines a five-step continuous risk-management process. The process begins with a mission but could also begin with a make-or-buy decision or new service request.

Steps one and two constitute risk assessment. Joint doctrine stresses the importance of determining the root cause or causes of each hazard, in step one, to improve the effectiveness of risk controls. Absent a clear understanding of causality, the Army might choose

Figure S.1
Five-Step Risk Management Process

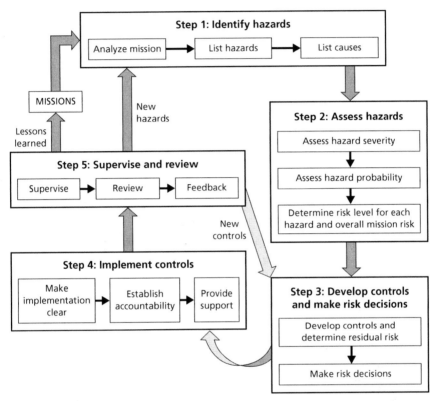

SOURCES: Department of the Army (1998b); Department of the Army et al. (2001).
RAND *MG282-S.1*

the wrong control, which could be ineffective or harmful. Ideally, step two would include estimation of both the probability and severity of a potential loss. Army and joint doctrine provide a ranking matrix, which can facilitate the systematic evaluation of risks and the establishment of priorities quantitatively or qualitatively.

Risk mitigation, which occurs in steps three, four, and five, would involve developing a strategy for eliminating, reducing, or coping with risk. Step three calls for a determination of residual risk. By implication, the goal of developing risk controls is not necessarily to eliminate risk. It may be preferable for the Army to accept some amount of residual risk and develop a response and recovery plan.

Applying Risk Management Principles to the BSC

We apply the following definitions and methodologies to the BSC.

Listing Potential Hazards and Addressing Causality. We find that some potential hazards relate to the performance of specific activities, such as food service, transportation, etc., and others relate to higher-order concerns, such as mission success, force management, and security, defined as the safety of personnel, property, and information. However, a list of potential hazards, absent further analysis, is of little practical value. To design appropriate risk-mitigation strategies, the Army must also assess the hazards' underlying causality, probability, and severity. In tracing the origins of three hypothetical BSC failures, we find that problems can arise from poorly framed requests for services, trade-offs between quality and cost, and inadequate planning and coordination, but not necessarily from the decision to contract per se. Moreover, we find that the proximate cause of the failure is rarely the same as the underlying or root cause.

Evaluating Risk-Management Strategies and Tools in the BSC. We find that most risk management appears to have occurred during the source-selection process or within the structure and operation of the contract.

The BSC request for proposal, which calls for explicit consideration of performance risk in selecting a contractor, presents the most visible example of risk assessment. Moreover, we see evidence of efforts to address risk in ongoing decisions about sourcing new work, as occur through the JARB validation and source-selection processes. We see little evidence of formal risk assessment in the initial decision to reobtain contract support in the Balkans in 1998. However, the concept of "initial" is muddy because the BSC emerged from two previous contracts.

For the most part, the contract's risk-mitigation tools reside in its structure and operating principles. The BSC attempts to balance concerns about preparedness and flexibility through its preplanned performance-based work scope, IDIQ specification, and CPAF payment structure. The contract's built-in management and oversight mechanisms can also mitigate risk. Data reports provide a nearly continuous flow of information, potentially serving as an early warning system. The work order, funding, and award fee processes also provide opportunities to evaluate performance. In addition, the JARB's source-selection process may mitigate some cost- and quality-related performance risks by posing the option of alternative suppliers and inducing competition. Risk-mitigation tools may also have been introduced before the contract took effect, in the design of the source-selection criteria and process. The Army weighted experience and past performance heavily in the competition, contributing to the selection of a known and trusted quantity—the incumbent.

Day-to-day communication is another risk-mitigation tool in the BSC. The Army describes the benefits of developing "habitual relationships" with service providers, to establish a close, cooperative Army-contractor work environment and build confidence in each other's ability to perform. Finally, internal and external evaluations and audits, such as the U.S. General Accounting Office (GAO) reports, which are discussed below, can also mitigate risk.

Examining the BSC Track Record. We examine the BSC track record in light of the five-step risk-management process, focusing on reported concerns about performance and security. Three frequently cited GAO reports address performance in terms of costs, quality of life, and readiness. Concerns about security have tended to relate to the safety and protection of contract employees. More recently, attention has turned to the troops' safety, as it relates to the use of contractors and their employees.

The first GAO report addresses four specific instances of possible cost excesses, one relating to firefighting services, another to power generation, a third to base camp personalization, and a fourth to furniture orders. In all but one case, the proximate cause of the excess is an action taken by the contractor. In all cases, however, the root cause derives from either a planning and coordination problem or an incentives problem, typically involving both the contractor and the customer. With one exception, the costs appear to have been modest, especially in relation to total contract spending. In all cases, the excesses appear to have been amenable to timely correction.

Apparently in response to GAO's concerns, the Army took several steps to reduce costs. The Army's actions may suggest the merit of the concerns. However, the question remains as to the appropriate balance between cost and other objectives. For example, additional Army manpower and leadership focus might be needed to reduce costs. Given competing demands on these resources, the Army might choose to pay a premium to free them for other purposes. The Army's priorities might also shift over time from getting the job done at the start of an operation to cost after conditions have stabilized. Indeed, by adopting a "best value" source-selection process, the Army clearly indicated that cost was not its primary consideration.

The second GAO report addresses quality, concluding, "The vast majority of soldiers we surveyed said the Army's efforts [including the BSC] met or exceeded their quality of life expectations." And, providing an indication of overall BSC satisfaction, KBR typically receives "excellent" or better performance ratings.

The third GAO report raises general concerns about readiness, which we discuss in terms of the contractor's ability or willingness to respond when needed or called on. For the most part, the contractor appears to be reliable and responsive. However, looking beyond the BSC—e.g., to KBR's pre-BSC Balkans experience and to more recent events in Afghanistan and Iraq—we note that start-ups may pose additional challenges, not necessarily because of the use of contracts per se but because of more onerous planning, coordination, and management requirements, some relating to funding and security. We address concerns about security below.

To conclude the discussion of performance, one arena in which the risks associated with contracting appear to be very different from those associated with organic provision is consideration of the chain of command. Neither the contractor nor its employees fall under the military chain of command. Authority flows from the contract, through the contracting officer, to the contractor.

Regarding security, we have seen little evidence of risks relating to the safety of contract employees or troops in the BSC, but violence, injuries, and death elsewhere demonstrate the prevalence of significant risks in other, less stable operating environments. The extent to which safety might affect the willingness of a contract provider and its employees to work, hence feeding back to readiness, would likely depend on their perception of the risk, their tolerance for risk, and the compensation that the Army offers them for taking the risk. Such considerations may be negotiable in some circumstances and can, potentially, be addressed in the terms of a contract.

Conclusions and Lessons Learned

We began by asking three questions: Is the Army getting what it needs from its CSS contracts? Do those contracts present any unrecognized, unmitigated, or unnecessary risks? If the Army is not getting what it needs or is accepting inappropriate risks, what can it do about it? On the basis of the BSC, it would appear that the Army has been getting what it needs, though it may, at times, have accepted more cost-related risk than necessary to get it. Moreover, the large number of contract participants and organizations may pose additional risks in terms of challenges in planning, coordination, and management. Short tours and abbreviated training for some government contracting and functional personnel and end users might compound those risks.

Nevertheless, the BSC appears to have delivered as promised, insofar as its developers sought to implement a high-quality contract and, at least initially, to deemphasize cost. Whether the Army accepted too much cost-based risk at the outset of the operations remains an open question, given the totality of its objectives and the evolving nature of contract management. Regarding readiness, the BSC appears to be a reliable and responsive arrangement, judging from its performance in the context of an ongoing operation. In terms of higher-order concerns, the BSC also appears to be a relatively safe arrangement. However, drawing a larger circle to include the pre-BSC experience under LOGCAP and other, more recent CSS activities in Afghanistan, Iraq, and elsewhere, we see evidence of risks to readiness and security.

To conclude, we draw together and highlight some of the key findings of this report to make three general points, which are applicable to other CSS contracts, even those providing different types of services.

First, not all risks in the BSC are inherently contractual. The discussion of hypothetical BSC failures and the contract's track record suggest that relatively few risks arise directly—or only—from the decision to contract. Rather, most are inherent in particular activities or the operating environment. Indeed, a contract may provide an effective vehicle for addressing risk through its structure, including its management and oversight mechanisms.

Second, a contract is only as good as its customer. The customer—and those acting on the customer's behalf—must possess the ability to plan, coordinate, and manage the contract. To the extent that performance-based contracts, particularly those involving wide-ranging participation, require special skills, DoD contracting and functional personnel and Army and other end users might require additional training.

Third, risk management is not risk elimination. A commander obviously wants to anticipate hazards and reduce or avoid the risks associated with them whenever it is practical, but, to achieve the Army's primary objectives in the theater, it may be necessary to accept some risk. It may also be necessary to balance risks across competing objectives. This logic applies as well to the use of contractors as it does to any other aspect of operational command.

Acknowledgments

The Assistant Deputy Assistant Secretary of the Army for Manpower and Reserve Affairs, John C. Anderson, was the Army project officer for this work and took an active interest in its execution throughout. He provided useful ideas, references, and support, as did Eileen G. Ginsburg from his office. Thomas J. Edwards, Deputy to the Commanding General of the U.S. Army Combined Arms Support Command (CASCOM), and Gordon L. Campbell, CASCOM's Principal Deputy to the Commanding General for Acquisition, provided valuable inputs and support. Robert W. Gruber, Jr., A. Brian Brobson, and their staff at the U.S. Army Corps of Engineers Transatlantic Programs Center provided detailed information about the BSC and, more generally, Army contracting in support of deployed forces.

We received valuable feedback during multiple presentations based on the material in this report in the Office of the Assistant Secretary of the Army for Manpower and Reserve Affairs; Headquarters, Department of the Army; Headquarters, Training and Doctrine Command; Headquarters, Army Materiel Command; and CASCOM. Personnel in many other parts of the Army helped us better understand how the Army uses contractors to support deployed forces.

Bruce Orvis, director of the Arroyo Center Manpower and Training Program, supported and reviewed the work. John Bondanella, Brent Fulton, and Ellen Pint, who were studying minimum military-essential logistics capabilities in the Arroyo Center's Military Logistics Program, were generous with their data, contacts, and insights. Ellen Pint and Susan Gates also provided formal reviews, which yielded significant improvements in the quality and accessibility of the overall report. Gail Kouril helped us find a wide variety of sources relevant to contracting on the battlefield. Discussions with other RAND colleagues provided useful insights, as did discussions with Steven H. Sternlieb of the U.S. General Accounting Office (now the Government Accountability Office), and with members of the KBR management team. Michael J. Meese of the U.S. Military Academy provided especially helpful comments on a related presentation at the Western Economics Association meetings held in July 2003. Chip Leonard of RAND read earlier drafts closely and helped improve them.

We thank them all but retain responsibility for the accuracy of the findings reported and our conclusions.

Abbreviations

ACO	Administrative contracting officer
AFDO	Award Fee Determining Official
AFDP	Award Fee Determining Plan
AFEB	Award Fee Evaluation Board
AO	Area of operations
AOR	Area of responsibility
ASG	Area Support Group
BCA	Board of Contract Appeals
BCCA	Base Camp Coordinating Agency
BRS	Brown and Root Services
BSC	Balkans Support Contract
CASCOM	Combined Arms Support Command
CDRL	Contract data requirements list
CETAC	U.S. Army Corp of Engineers, Transatlantic Programs Center
CLIN	Contract line-item number
CO	Contracting officer
COR	Contracting officer representative
CPAF	Cost plus award fee
CR	Central Region

CSS	Combat service support
DCAA	Defense Contract Audit Agency
DCMA	Defense Contract Management Agency
DCMD	Defense Contract Management District
DCS	Deputy Chief of Staff
DLA	Defense Logistics Agency
DoD	U.S. Department of Defense
DPW	Directorate of Public Works
FY	Fiscal year
GAO	U.S. General Accounting Office (now the Government Accountability Office)
HAZMAT	Hazardous material
HWSA	Hazardous waste storage area
IC	Installation coordinator
IDIQ	Indefinite delivery, indefinite quantity
JARB	Joint Acquisitions Review Board
JCC	Joint Contracting Center
KBR	Kellogg Brown and Root
LOE	Level of effort
LOGCAP	Logistics Civil Augmentation Program
MIPR	Military Interdepartmental Purchase Request
MOU	Memorandum of understanding
NTP	Notice to proceed
OJFS	Operation Joint Forge Sustainment
PCO	Principal contracting officer
PE	Performance evaluator
RFP	Request for proposal
ROM	Rough order of magnitude

SEAhut	Southeast Asia hut
SSA	Source Selection Authority
SSAC	Source Selection Advisory Council
SSEB	Source-Selection Evaluation Board
TA	Taszar Airfield
TAC	Transatlantic Programs Center
TO	Theater of operations
TSB	Taszar Support Base
TF	Task force
USAREUR	U.S. Army Europe
USACE	U.S. Army Corps of Engineers
WBS	Work breakdown structure

CHAPTER ONE

Introduction

Contractors provide the Army with services in a wide variety of settings, including classrooms, recruiting stations, international counternarcotics operations, and peacekeeping missions. Overseas settings, particularly at or near the battlefield, are among the most controversial. Recent pressures on the Army to rely more heavily on contractors and the increasingly ill-defined nature of the battlefield raise serious questions for policymakers. Is the Army getting what it needs from its combat service support (CSS) contracts? Do those contracts present any unrecognized, unmitigated, or unnecessary risks? If the Army is not getting what it needs or is accepting inappropriate risks, what can it do about it?

Case studies of CSS contracts can provide some answers to these questions. In this report, we present a case study of the Balkans Support Contract (BSC), a CSS contract that has involved deployment. We chose the BSC because of its extensive track record, scope, and size. The contract has provided wide-ranging life support, transportation, and maintenance services to the Army and other end users over several years in a dynamic operating environment. Moreover, it is likely the largest CSS contract in the Balkans and among the largest in the world. Although officially the BSC augments Army military support capabilities in the Balkans and nearby countries—e.g., Bosnia, Hungary, Kosovo—it has helped the Army reduce its in-house role in CSS provision in the region by partially devolving responsibilities for service coordination and delivery and freeing up resources, especially Army manpower, for other core functions.

However, we also recognize the limitations of applying lessons learned from the BSC to other contracts. For example, the BSC has its roots in earlier contracts and so some lessons learned may not be relevant to start-ups. Strictly speaking, the BSC has been operating in the Balkans region only since 1999. However, its history dates back to the start of the Army's first Logistics Civil Augmentation Program (LOGCAP) umbrella contract. LOGCAP is a U.S. Army initiative for peacetime planning for the use of civilian contractors in wartime and other contingencies.

Another, more obvious limitation is that, while the BSC provides wide-ranging life support, transportation, and maintenance services, it does not provide all types of services. For example, the BSC is not a weapon system support contract and so our analysis does not address risks that may be specific to such contracts.

Nevertheless, the BSC's track record, scope, and size offer insight into many of the risks associated with contracting in deployment and the approaches used to manage them. By analyzing the performance of the contract through the lens of risk management, consisting of risk assessment and mitigation, we draw lessons for U.S. policymakers, especially those involved in contracting, force structure, or military operations and support planning processes. In so doing, we also compare some of the risks of different sources. We undertake this analysis of the BSC by examining official contracting records, previous studies, and press reports and by interviewing customers, contractors, and other observers.

This report proceeds in three additional chapters. First, we describe the origins and key characteristics of the BSC, including U.S. Department of Defense (DoD) agencies' roles in management and oversight and the contract's structure and operating mechanisms. This description provides much of the data for the analysis of the BSC that follows in the subsequent chapter. Second, we present a five-step process for assessing and mitigating risk. We use the framework, along with another risk-management methodology known as a "fault-tree," to evaluate the BSC, including both its development and implementation. The five-step process draws directly from Army and joint doctrine. Third, we report conclusions and lessons learned.

CHAPTER TWO

Origins and Characteristics of the BSC

This chapter describes the origins and characteristics of the BSC. It provides much of the data for the authors' analysis, using the risk-management framework. We explicitly address the contract's origins and characteristics—the data—through the lens of that framework in subsequent chapters.

The BSC is an umbrella contract that offers life support, transportation, maintenance, and other CSS in the Balkans region and involves participants, including government contracting and functional personnel drawn from several DoD agencies, various end users, and a contractor and its employees spanning countries and continents. U.S. Army Europe (USAREUR) funds the contract, and deployed U.S. forces in Bosnia, Hungary, and Kosovo are among the end users. Other end users include NATO allies and multinational stabilization forces. The U.S. Army Corp of Engineers, Transatlantic Programs Center (CETAC) administers the contract from Winchester, Virginia, and provides the principal contracting officer (PCO). Other U.S. government agencies, such as the Defense Contract Management Agency (DCMA), also contribute administrative support, including field-level administrative contracting officers (ACOs).[1] Halliburton KBR Government Operations, formerly known as Brown and Root Services (BRS), is the contractor.[2]

---

[1] DCMA replaced the Defense Contract Management Command (DCMC).

[2] According to a Halliburton press release, dated December 17, 2001, Halliburton KBR Government Operations was formerly known as Brown and Root Services. KBR stands for

KBR is only one of more than 100 contractors operating in the region but clearly is among the most important. In 2000, the U.S. General Accounting Office (GAO) described the BSC as the largest single contract in the Balkans.[3] Despite projected cost declines for FY 2003 and FY 2004, the contract will most likely remain the region's largest. The costs of CSS under the BSC have amounted to hundreds of million of dollars annually (see Table 2.1).[4]

The performance of the BSC largely derives from the intent, design, and implementation of earlier CSS contracts, including the Army's first comprehensive LOGCAP umbrella contract, which predates the BSC contract award and even the Balkans operations.

Given the inherent uncertainties of operating in contingency environments, the Army has sought to balance potentially competing demands for preparedness and responsiveness, along with its apparent interest in reducing its role in CSS provision in the region, relating to end-strength and various other resource constraints. The BSC, like its predecessors, was set up as a preplanned, performance-based, indefi-

Table 2.1
Total BSC Contract Costs

Fiscal Year	$ Millions
1999	410.5
2000	454.8
2001	415.5
2002	318.4
2003	273.3 (e)
2004	232.5 (e)
Total	2,105.0

SOURCE: CETAC records, provided May 2003.
NOTE: e = estimate.

Kellogg Brown and Root. At the time of the BSC award, the KBR was still known as BRS. For simplicity, we refer to the firm as "KBR" throughout the report.

[3] GAO (2000a, p. 3) refers to the BSC as "the largest contract for services to U.S. forces." GAO (2000a, p. 5) further reports, "The Army contracts with more than 100 firms to obtain goods and services in the Balkans. The largest single contract is the Balkans Support Contract."

[4] Contract costs also appear in GAO (2000a, p. 9). GAO presents annual estimates of contract costs but does not compare them to the costs of equivalent organic support.

nite delivery, indefinite quantity (IDIQ) contract, with a cost-plus-award-fee (CPAF) payment structure. As we discuss later in this report, this formulation promotes readiness through advanced preparation but is especially flexible and requires less micromanagement than other cost-based formulations. However, the BSC is by no means self-governing or free of management responsibilities.

Origins

We begin the BSC chronology in the early 1990s and describe some of the most significant contract-related events leading up to its implementation in 1999.

KBR won the Army's first comprehensive LOGCAP umbrella contract in August 1992. Under that contract, KBR provided multifunctional services to the Army at various sites worldwide, eventually including the Balkans in 1995, and established the foundation for a continuing CSS relationship with the Army. The contract included a one-year base period and four one-year renewal periods. The fundamental concepts guiding the development of the LOGCAP program have been to[5]

- plan during peacetime for the effective use of contractor support in contingency or crisis;
- leverage existing global and regional corporate resources as facility and logistics service support multipliers;
- provide an alternative capability to meet facility and logistic services shortfalls; and
- provide quick reaction to contingency or crisis requirements.

---

[5] Army Regulation 700-137 authorized the "LOGCAP" program in December 1985, but it was not until 1992 that USACE developed the first comprehensive umbrella contract, "a LOGCAP initiative for a single, worldwide, services contract to preplan for theater facilities and logistic support services in times of war or crisis." See USACE (1994, p. 2). In this report, we refer only to the umbrella-type contract, which took shape in 1992. The "fundamental concepts" appear in USACE (1994, p. 3).

The LOGCAP contract presents an opportunity to fill requirements externally through a designated contractor, but not an obligation. It is a standing arrangement that the Army can activate as needed. On that basis, KBR entered the Balkans in November 1995 to help support contingency operations there.[6]

In 1997, when the first LOGCAP contract expired, the Army chose to replace KBR with DynCorp but opted to retain KBR's services in the Balkans.[7] To that end, CETAC awarded KBR a separate sole-source contract, or "spinoff," known as Operation Joint Forge Sustainment (OJFS) and valued at about $400 million in total.[8] The term of the sole-source OJFS contract ran for two years, from May 1997 to May 1999, during which time KBR provided the same or similar services as it had under LOGCAP, according to the same or similar guiding principles.[9] GAO (2000a, p. 6), states the reasons for the Army's decision to award a sole-source contract to KBR:

- The contractor had already acquired the knowledge of how to operate within the laws and regulations of the countries in which it was providing support.
- The contractor had demonstrated the ability to support the operation.
- Changing contractors would have generated additional costs for such activities as personnel duplication required for the transition between contractors.

---

[6] We discuss the locations of the operations and the services provided in later chapters of this report.

[7] Also in that time frame—i.e., October 1, 1996—governance of the LOGCAP contract shifted from USACE to the U.S. Army Materiel Command (Kolar, 1997), but the Balkans contract remained with USACE, more specifically, with CETAC.

[8] Wynn (2000, p. 3) reports the value as $413.5 million.

[9] In comparing the LOGCAP contract, the OJFS contract, and the BSC, CETAC (1999a) finds that, "Excluding the worldwide planning portion of the LOGCAP contract, the scope of work and procedures are nearly identical for all three contracts."

In August 1998, as the expiration of the OJFS contract approached, CETAC announced its intent to issue a request for proposal (RFP) for the next Balkans contract, thus initiating an open competition.[10] Although CETAC approached the selection process for the new contract differently, the operating concept remained largely unchanged. CETAC awarded the contract under consideration in this report, the BSC, to KBR in February 1999 for a five-year term. The term commenced with a one-year base period, which ran from May 1999 to May 2000. The BSC continues to operate under a set of one-year option periods, scheduled to end in May 2004.[11]

CETAC selected KBR for "best value," basing the decision on four evaluation factors, consisting of the management and execution plan, experience, past performance, and cost. (See Box 2.1.) The three factors other than cost were to be weighed equally and, in combination, were to be considered "significantly more important" than the single cost factor. The RFP stressed that a cheaper proposal would not necessarily be viewed as a better proposal. Indeed, the cost factor did not refer to cost "level" per se; rather it addressed "realism," "completeness," and "financial capability." Nevertheless, some of the other factors included cost-related references, potentially providing an opening for further consideration. For example, in the context of the more process-oriented management and execution plan criteria, the RFP asked bidders to "describe your overall plan for accomplishing this project in the most cost-effective and efficient manner." Finally, performance risk was to be assessed for all four factors, but not separately.[12]

---

[10] See CETAC (1998a).

[11] At the time of this writing, information about follow-on activities was not yet available.

[12] We address this aspect of the selection process in a later discussion of risk mitigation.

BOX 2.1
SOURCE-SELECTION CRITERIA

The RFP describes a "best value" source-selection process, clearly emphasizing "non-cost" factors. The RFP also draws attention to performance risk, by calling for its consideration with respect to all factors, but it does not explain how it will be accomplished.[a]

"Award will be made to the responsible offeror whose proposal contains the combination of those criteria offering the best overall value to the Government. This will be determined by comparing the difference in the value of technical (non-cost) features of proposals with the difference in cost to the Government. In making the comparison the Government is more concerned with obtaining superior technical or management features than with making an award at the lowest overall cost to the Government. However, the Government will not make an award at a significantly higher overall cost to the Government to achieve slightly superior technical or management features. All evaluation factors other than cost or price, when combined, are significantly more important than cost or price. Fee will not be an evaluation factor. Though not separately established as an evaluation factor, Performance Risk (understanding the scope; risk to the successful performance of the contract) will be considered with respect to all factors. ...[The] Government prefers to obtain better offeror past performance, experience and a better management and execution plan rather than to obtain relatively small price savings."

The emphasis on noncost factors does not imply that cost is not a factor in source selection. From the RFP, "This is a Best Value source selection... Although cost is of significantly lesser importance than the aggregate [w]eight of the non-cost evaluation factors, it is an important factor and should not be ignored." The RFP lists specific evaluation factors and subfactors as follows, explaining, "All non-cost factors are considered of equal importance":[b]

- Management/Execution Plan, including
  — Execution plan
  — Manpower utilization plan
  — Key personnel
  — Program management controls
  — Cost control management plan
  — Plan for management of subcontractors
- Experience, including experience with
  — Supplies and services contracts, especially broad-spectrum logistics support to deployed military forces or remotely stationed customers and/or at multiple sites
  — Contracts in Europe and especially the Balkans region
  — Cost reimbursable contracts
  — Operation and maintenance of military infrastructure
  — The design and performance of minor construction and repair projects
- Past Performance
- Cost, including
  — Realism[c]
  — Completeness
  — Financial capability

BOX 2.1—CONTINUED

The RFP also calls for an oral presentation, but it is not subject to separate evaluation.

SOURCE: Balkans Support Contract, Request for Proposal, October 9, 1998.
[a] The source-selection plan issued to evaluators provides additional information.
[b] The RFP includes additional, more detailed criteria for each factor and subfactor.
[c] Section L of the RFP indicates that evaluators will conduct a cost realism analysis. Moreover, Section M indicates the importance of realism in other dimensions also, "Proposals unrealistic in terms of technical approach, management commitment, or cost will be deemed indicative of an inherent lack of comprehension of the complexity and risks of the requirements, and may be rejected."

The selection process included participants from the U.S. Army Corp of Engineers, USAREUR, and the Defense Logistics Agency (DLA), together forming a set of specialized committees for each factor, an evaluation board, and an advisory council.[13] The Source Selection Authority (SSA), in this case the CETAC contracting officer, made the final decision based on their input. Figure 2.1 depicts the organizational structure of the source selection process.

As stated in the Source-Selection Plan, all three of the evaluation committees evaluated the contractor's proposals against the criteria established in the RFP for their particular area, but only the noncost committees developed point scores.[14] Next, the Source-Selection Evaluation Board (SSEB) established the weights for each evaluation criterion and applied them to the point scores. The Source-Selection Advisory Council (SSAC) acted as a buffer between the SSEB and the SSA, resolving disputes, ensuring that evaluations were performed in accordance with the source-selection criteria in the solicitation, evalu-

---

[13] The DLA participants came from DCMC's Defense Contract Management District International (DCMD-I), which has since been replaced by DCMA—now separate from DLA—and DCMA International (DCMA-I).

[14] CETAC staff provided an undated copy of the plan. It was used in 1998 in the source-selection process. Per contracting guidance, cost did not receive a point score. "Cost/price shall not be scored or otherwise combined with other aspects of the technical proposal evaluation. No predetermined formulas may be used, although the cost or price may be used to evaluate an offeror's understanding of the RFP scope of work" (CETAC-OC, 1997, pp. 37–38).

Figure 2.1
Source-Selection Organizational Structure

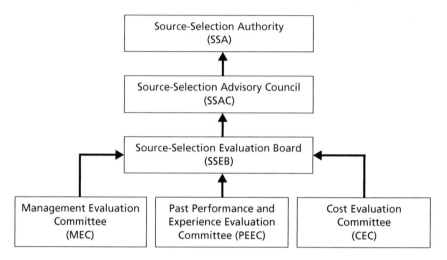

SOURCE: Source Selection Plan.
RAND MG282-2.1

ating the SSEB's recommendation for award, and processing the award recommendations to the SSA. The SSAC was authorized to prepare a written minority opinion if it did not agree with SSEB's recommendation, which it would send back to the SSEB for further evaluation.

The BSC competition was open but ultimately thin. Although several firms displayed interest in the RFP at the outset—five participated in a site visit—the competition ended with a choice between KBR and just one other firm. Why? The experience factor may have had a winnowing effect, perhaps intentionally so. In particular, the RFP sought experience with

- supplies and services contracts, especially broad-spectrum logistics support to deployed military forces or remotely stationed customers and/or at multiple sites;
- contracts in Europe and especially the Balkans region;
- cost reimbursable contracts;
- operation and maintenance of military infrastructure; and

- the design and performance of minor construction and repair projects.

On the basis of those criteria, and recalling the Army's reported justification for awarding the sole-source contract in 1997—particularly acquired knowledge and demonstrated ability—it is hard to imagine a firm other than KBR winning the BSC. At the time of the competition, KBR was already a long-standing CSS provider under a cost reimbursable contract—i.e., LOGCAP. From FY 1992 to FY 1996, KBR serviced operations in Somalia, Rwanda, Haiti, Saudi Arabia and Kuwait, and Italy under LOGCAP. Those early efforts were modest in comparison to the BSC but still significant, with costs totaling well over $200 million (see Table 2.2). Per the call for familiarity with "contracts in Europe and *especially* the Balkans region," KBR also had pre-BSC experience in the Balkans. From FY 1996 to FY 1998, the Army spent about $775 million on KBR's services in the region.

Table 2.2
Estimates of LOGCAP Contract Costs, FY 1993–FY 1996

| | Cost Estimates in $ Millions | | |
Country/Operation	CETAC	GAO (1997)	GAO (2000)
Somalia/Restore Hope (FY 1993–1994)	107.3	62.0	NA
Rwanda/Support Hope (FY 1994)	6.3	6.3	NA
Haiti/Uphold Democracy (FY 1994– 1995)	150.1	133.0	NA
Saudi Arabia and Kuwait/Vigilant Warrior (FY 1995)	5.0	5.1	NA
Somalia/Restore Hope (FY 1995)	2.4	NA	NA
Italy/Deny Flight (FY 1996)	6.3	6.3	NA
Pre-BSC Balkans Support (FY 1996– 1998)	NA	NA	776.4
Total	277.4	212.7	776.4

SOURCES: CETAC (1999a); GAO (2000a) for pre-BSC Balkans support; and GAO (1997) for other data.
NOTE: Not all sources provide operation names or dates. GAO does not separately identify spending on Operation Restore Hope in FY 1995. GAO indicates that spending on Operation Deny Flight began in FY 1995—i.e., September 1995. The figure for pre-BSC Balkans support includes costs incurred under the sole-source contract.

KBR's pre-BSC—and pre-Balkans—experience is relevant to the BSC risk analysis for several reasons: first, it implies the Army and KBR had an established relationship before the BSC award, presumably resulting in some degree of trust; second, it implies KBR was acquainted with the particular rigors and needs of the region, which was cited as a justification for the sole-source award in 1997 and then included as an experience criterion for the BSC competition; third, it implies KBR was also acquainted with the contract type. All factors combined, KBR, as a known quantity, would likely raise fewer concerns about performance in the Balkans region than would a new entrant in the market, but, at the same time, the competition could create incentives for KBR to be more cost conscious.

However, KBR's pre-BSC track record also implies that the BSC experience, if defined solely by the 1999 contract, may not speak to the full range of risks in other venues. For example, the start-up of the 1999 contract would say little about the start-up of an entirely new venture. The implementation of the LOGCAP contract in the Balkans in late 1995 might offer more insight but still would be of limited value in identifying the pitfalls of a "cold start," as preplanning and experience likely facilitated it, as intended.

Key Characteristics

The BSC, like its predecessors, is a preplanned, performance-based, IDIQ contract, with a CPAF payment structure.[15] What does this mean? First, a performance-based contract tells the contractor what the customer wants done but does not tell the contractor how to do it. In the BSC, the work scope and associated work breakdown structures (WBSs) list both broad requirements and particular types of services, framed in terms of outcomes not processes. From Federal Acquisition Regulation 37.6 (a), performance-based contracting methods: "Describe the requirements in terms of results required

---

[15] The following descriptions draw heavily from CETAC (2001b) and other Army documents.

rather than the methods of performance of the work."[16] In principle, a performance-based contract may define "what" in considerable detail, but only as needed to communicate the requirement.

From the Armed Services Board of Contract Appeals (BCA) 14447, 72-2 BCA, paragraph 9626:

> Performance specifications set forth operational characteristics desired for the item. In such specifications design, measurements and other specific details are not stated nor considered important so long as the performance requirement is met. Where an item is purchased by a performance specification, the contractor accepts general responsibility for design, engineering and achievement of the stated performance requirements. The contractor has general discretion and election as to detail but the work is subject to the Government's reserved right to final inspection and approval or rejection. (CETAC, 2002b.)

With a performance-based contract, the contractor can respond more rapidly to new opportunities and challenges as they arise.[17] For example, if low-cost labor is readily available, the contractor can substitute workers for machinery. If the labor pool shrinks, the contractor can try to shift the mix. The ability to change "how" implies that the Army can also leverage the contractor's know-how as it grows with experience and benefit from newly emerging best commercial practices.

Second, an IDIQ contract does not specify the delivery date or exact quantities at the time of the award. This level of generality is desirable when the customer lacks information about "when" or "how much" prior to the start of an operation or expects significant but unpredictable changes in requirements over the life of the operation. As needs become known, the customer obtains services through task orders.

---

[16] Reprinted in CETAC (2002b).

[17] As we discuss below, the CPAF payment structure, if based on the negotiated estimated cost, can provide incentives both to improve the quality of service delivery and reduce costs.

As "preplanned" implies, the contractor develops an implementation plan for a future contingency, whether the operation is announced or hypothetical, as in a LOGCAP regional plan. The plan typically covers the full range of potential activities posited in the work scope and WBSs. In the BSC, this plan is known as the "Management and Execution Plan." It includes the

- execution plan,
- manpower utilization plan,
- key personnel,
- program management controls,
- cost control management plan, and
- plan for management of subcontractors.

In general, beyond the basic outline, the content of a plan depends on many factors, including the extent to which the customer can anticipate its needs—or the possible range of its needs. This does not mean that less planning will occur in a highly uncertain world, only that the plan needs to be tailored to deal with the uncertainty. Indeed, there may be even more planning to prepare for a broad spectrum of possible and potentially changing needs. For example, the contractor may create an especially wide-ranging "Rolodex" of employee candidates, only some of whom might be called on. In the case of the BSC, the contractor, KBR, provided a high level of resolution, with details on process and substance, drawing heavily from its experience serving the Army in the area of operation and elsewhere.

Third, a CPAF contract reimburses costs within certain agreed-on limits, typically guarantees a set base fee, and provides performance incentives through award fees. In effect, the contractor makes its best effort to complete the work within the negotiated estimated cost. If the contractor exceeds that cost—a ceiling—without permission from the contracting officer, it does so at its own risk.[18] In return, the

---

[18] Technically, the contractor can exceed the cost ceiling, but the Army customer need not count any costs above the ceiling as allowable and so reimbursable—in fact, the customer cannot obligate above the ceiling without a formal contract modification.

customer agrees to reimburse all incurred costs deemed "allocable, allowable, and reasonable" and to pay base and, possibly, award fees. Wynn (2000, p. 6) explains allocable, allowable, and reasonable in layman's terms:

- A cost is reasonable if it does not exceed that which a prudent person would incur while conducting a competitive business.[19]
- A cost is allocable if it is incurred specifically for the contract or if it is necessary to the overall operation of the business.
- A cost is allowable if it is reasonable, allocable, meets the terms of the contract, and is not specifically disallowable. Some examples of disallowable costs are those incurred for entertainment, fines and penalties, and political activities.

Typically, a contract has a total ceiling, defined by the sum of the cost estimates associated with each of its parts, and separate ceilings for each of its parts, known as contract line-item numbers (CLINs). This means that a cost is allowable only so long as it does not exceed the lowest-level cost ceiling applied to it. By implication, the contractor cannot use an shortfall on one CLIN to offset an overage on another. Thus, the IDIQ CPAF structure allows considerable flexibility at a macro level, but it can also afford control and accountability at the CLIN level. However, the BSC appears to preserve CLIN-level flexibility by defining line items broadly, in terms of each of its task orders—e.g., CLIN 0001, "Home Office Support Services for Period May 28, 1999, through September 30, 1999."

The BSC specifies base and award fees as percentages of the negotiated *estimated* cost, not the actual cost. The distinction is important for its effect on the contractor's incentives. A contract with fees based on the negotiated estimated cost creates incentives for the

---

[19] Wynn (2000, p. 6) further elaborates on the concept of reasonableness: "What is reasonable depends on a variety of considerations, including whether the cost is recognized as ordinary and necessary for conducting business or performing tasks under the contract. Does the work meet acceptable sound business practices? Does it meet federal and state laws and regulations? Does the work significantly deviate from the contractor's established practices?"

contractor to negotiate the highest estimated cost possible, thereby inflating the base fee and possibly the award fee. As such, the burden is on the Army to negotiate judiciously. However, once the negotiation is complete, it creates incentives for the contractor to control actual costs, thereby increasing the rate of return on the contract and possibly the award fee. The base fee is automatic, but the award fee depends on the contractor's performance. (The incentive to reduce costs will be even stronger if cost is a factor in the award fee determination.) In the BSC, the base fee is 1 percent of the negotiated estimated cost and the award fee is *up to* 8 percent.[20] In the first LOGCAP contract, the base fee was also set at 1 percent, but separate award fees were established for planning, up to 5 percent, and execution, up to 9 percent.

A performance-based, IDIQ, CPAF contract can afford considerable flexibility to the customer and contractor and requires less micromanagement than many other types of contracts. However, this formulation is not self-governing or without management rights and responsibilities.[21] Indeed, management rights and responsibilities begin with the earliest phases of planning and carry over into daily operations. For example, in requesting new services, the customer must evaluate the contractor's proposal, including the concept of operation. The customer also has the right to final inspection and approval or rejection of the work product, as noted in the BCA excerpt. Moreover, the BSC offers built-in management and oversight mechanisms. A CETAC briefing (2001a) lists several "Controls Over Contractor," including the award fee process, limitations of funds and costs letters, and the contract data requirements list (CDRL).

---

[20] The 1 percent base fee and 8 percent award fee were placed on the RFP and carried over into the award. See CETAC (2001b, FAQ 10), "Why does the contract provide for a 1% base and 8% award fee?" The percentages were not subject to negotiation. See RFP, Section B, "Supplies or Services and Prices/Costs," p. B-1, note 1.

[21] In a comparison of cost-based and fixed-price contracts, Wynn (2000, p. 5) notes, "cost contracts require intensive oversight by the government to identify and constrain scope of work creep and cost growth in a timely manner."

In the following sections, we provide more detail on key DoD agencies' roles in management and oversight and the contract's operating mechanisms.

DoD Agencies' Roles in Management and Oversight

Managing and overseeing the BSC involves many people and organizations. In addition to USAREUR—the bill-payer—several other DoD agencies have formal governance roles (see Table 2.3). The need for close coordination among them may create management and oversight challenges. As previously noted, CETAC administers the BSC from Winchester, Virginia, and provides the PCO. Other agencies, such as DCMA and the Defense Contract Audit Agency (DCAA), also participate. For example, DCMA supplies contract administration personnel, including the ACOs, quality assurance specialists, property administrators, and other specialists to help monitor costs, typically on six-month field rotations and, more recently, with overlapping terms (GAO, 2000a, pp. 10 and 24–25, and conversations with CETAC in 2002). The ACOs and their contracting officer representatives (CORs) provide a formal field-level link between the contractor and its customer. DCMA trains the CORs, which are drawn from the deployed task forces and from Area Support Groups (see discussion below).

Contracting officers serve an essential chain of command function. They have the legal authority to enter into, administer, and terminate contracts (Department of the Army, 2003, pp. 1-4 and 1-5). In fact, a contracting officer is the only official who can issue performance directives to the contractor. By regulation, the "contracting officer is the only government official with the authority to increase, decrease, or materially alter a contract's scope of work" and the contractor will supervise and manage its employees (Department of the Army, 1999, p. 14). As such, task force (TF) commanders participate in management and oversight through the mechanisms shown in Table 2.3, but they have no direct control over contractors, such as KBR, or their employees.

Table 2.3
DoD Agencies' Responsibilities for Overseeing the BSC

Agency or Organization	Oversight Responsibilities
USAREUR DCS/Logistics	Develops and implements theater policies and procedures with USAREUR staff proponents Provides contract and program command integration Coordinates with CETAC and DCMA and hosts award fee evaluations Issues weekly analysis Holds approval authority for all new work valued at or above $50,000, all new recurring services, and exceptions to Red or Blue Book policies
CETAC	Awards contract Provides PCO Prepares contract modifications Processes contract billing Performs financial analysis
DCMA[a]	Provides contract administration services (on-site ACOs) Provides property administration Provides quality assurance Conducts cost and price validation
DCAA	Performs audits down range Performs incurred cost audits in the continental United States
TF commanders	Provide management and control in their areas of responsibility Work with budget targets Hold approval authority for new work less than $50,000

SOURCE: CETAC, 2003.
[a] Historically, DCMA, previously DCMC, has exercised the customer's right to approval or rejection of the work product, by "sign[ing] off on all completed work to ensure that the job was done according to the contract" (McElroy, 1999, p. 1).

In addition, Wynn (2000) describes the role of a once-prominent Base Camp Coordinating Agency (BCCA), which the Army assembled for the Balkans operations in January 1996. Initially, the BCCA performed many of the same functions as a directorate of public works (DPW) and assisted the ACOs with ensuring the quality of the contractor's construction. An early report from the Balkans describes the BCCA as "the focal point for building, sustaining, and decommissioning all U.S. base camps in Bosnia, Herzegovina, and Croatia" (Jones, 1997). The BCCA also ran training programs, coordinated town hall meetings, and participated in the review process for new service orders. However, as the Army gained more experience with the BSC, the full range of BCCA-provided services became less necessary.

In 2001, the Army approved the establishment of Area Support Groups (ASGs), as a new structure for command and control for base operations functions and Title 10 support services provided to U.S. military and civilian personnel deployed in the Balkans. The creation of the ASGs, which are subordinate units assigned to HQ USAREUR, relieved the deploying forces of the responsibility for supervising routine base operations and administrative control functions. According to the USAREUR commander's orders, the intent was to unburden the TF commander and his staff of base operations issues and increase his ability to focus on his stabilization force mission tasks. The ASGs effectively absorbed the BCCA's remaining responsibilities, especially its DPW functions.

Though not an "agency," strictly speaking, the Joint Acquisition Review Board (JARB) also plays a central role in contract management and oversight, specifically through the work order process.[22] The JARB consists of ASG and TF members and advisors, drawn from several military institutions (see Figure 2.4). It is responsible for validating certain requirements, making a best-value source selection, ensuring that inappropriate or unauthorized purchases are not processed, and documenting the validation and source-selection processes. As the reference to "source selection" implies, the BSC is not the only means by which the Army can obtain services in the Balkans. Indeed, the Army is expected to establish whether the BSC is the most appropriate source case by case. Like LOGCAP, the BSC establishes an opportunity to fill requirements but not an obligation.

We conclude this section with a discussion of a role that is neither "management" nor "oversight" per se but clearly bears on the functioning of the contract and the contract employees. Under the terms of the BSC, the government is responsible for providing the

---

[22] We discuss the functions of the JARB in more detail in a later discussion of work orders.

contractor and its employees with various types of support services, including medical services and force protection. Regarding force protection, the government must provide "necessary security for Contractor personnel throughout the Theater of Operation (TO). This includes but is not limited to the security of Contractor work sites, movement throughout the TO (i.e., between work sites and living and messing areas) and ingress and egress to the TO." On a day-to-day basis, this responsibility falls largely to the TF commanders.

The contractor is responsible for other aspects of physical security, possibly leaving room for confusion about the roles of the Army and the contractor in-theater and almost certainly suggesting a need for close coordination between them. Physical security is defined as, "that part of security concerned with the physical measures designed to safeguard personnel, to prevent unauthorized access to equipment, facilities, material and documents, and to safeguard them against espionage, sabotage, damage, and theft."[23] In particular, "The Contractor shall be responsible for physical security of all materials, supplies, and equipment of every description, including property that may be Government-furnished or owned, and all work performed, and also of areas occupied jointly by the Contractor and the Government."

As evidence of the potential for confusion, two noteworthy questions arose during the preproposal phases of the BSC competition about the limits of the contractor's responsibilities in-theater. One potential bidder asked whether it would be required to staff a guard force authorized to use deadly force. In a sharply worded response, the Army stressed that, "Contractors are ABSOLUTELY NOT allowed or authorized to use deadly force!" Another potential bidder asked whether it would be responsible for securing the camps.

---

[23] See RFP, 52.200-4061, "Responsibility for Physical Security," p. H-2, 5(1) and 5(2). Several other provisions also address other aspects of physical security. Sections 52.245-5 and 52.246-25, "Government Property" and "Limitation of Liability—Services," address government property security (pp. I-67 and I-71). Section 52.228-7001 addresses ground and flight risks (p. I-86). Section 52.228-7003 speaks to the government's responsibility for payments to contractors and their employees under conditions of capture or detention (p. I-89). Various provisions address hazardous waste and hazardous substance liability.

To which the Army replied less sharply, "No, the military does that, you are required to secure any government-furnished property and materials you possess in your work areas. The military secures the area."

The BSC's security provisions and the Army's responses to questions regarding "deadly force" are consistent with the guidance provided in the Army field manual, *Contractors on the Battlefield* (Department of the Army, 2003, p. 6-2). That manual places responsibility for protecting contractors and their employees squarely on the shoulders of the commander, but does not exclude the contractor entirely:

> Protecting contractors and their employees on the battlefield is the commander's responsibility. When contractors perform in potentially hostile or hazardous areas, the supported military forces must assure the protection of the operations and employees. The responsibility for assuring that contractors receive adequate force protection starts with the combatant commander, extends downward, and includes the contractor.

With regard to the responsibilities of the contractor:

> Contractors ensure that all of their employees follow all force protection requirements and supporting organization policies stated in the contract. Contractors (when required and authorized) should, as a minimum, ensure that their employees receive the directed NBC [nuclear, biological, and chemical] protection and weapons familiarization training. . . . Contractors are expected to take passive force protection measures for safety and security of their employees. Also contractors should mandate measures for self defense such as conducting driving classes, issuing cell phones, and establishing procedures for reporting suspicious incidents. (Department of the Army, 2003, p. 6-3.)

Any behaviors that might make the contractor's employees look more like soldiers and less like civilians could jeopardize their status as "civilians accompanying the force," which could put them at considerable additional risk in the event of attack or capture.[24] *Contractors on the Battlefield* sets out three conditions that make an individual a combatant:

- Being commanded and controlled by a published chain of command.
- Wearing distinctive insignia or uniform.
- Openly carrying arms. (Department of the Army, 2003, p. 2-12.)

The manual warns, "if the commander permits contractor employees to wear military-looking uniforms and carry weapons, he may jeopardize their status." Thus, the manual discourages such permission.[25]

Contract Structure and Operating Mechanism

Here, we describe the contract's structure and operating mechanisms, including the work scope and WBSs; the service order, work order, and funds administration processes; the award fee evaluation process; and the CDRL and other management and oversight tools.

---

[24] For more on contractor employees' status and the preservation of that status, see *Contractors on the Battlefield*, various chapters, including One, Two, Four, and Six. The manual states that contractor employees' status as civilians accompanying the force is clearly defined in the Geneva Conventions and other international agreements, conveying protection from intentional attack and entitlement to prisoner of war status, if captured. However, it also notes that their treatment will depend on the nature of the hostile force and their recognition, if any, of international law. It also describes some of the ways in which the contractor can jeopardize the status of its employees—e.g., by allowing them to carry arms or operate in direct support of military operations. For treatment of potential ambiguities regarding contractor employees' civilian status in contingency operations, see Department of the Army (1998a, p. 7).

[25] The Army does allow for the issuance of sidearms to contract employees for their personal self-defense. See Department of the Army (1998a, p. 3).

The Work Scope and WBS

The core of the BSC consists of a broadly written performance-based work scope with a set of WBSs. The contract is organized geographically, with categories of recurring services, such as base camp maintenance, laundry service, food service operations, equipment maintenance, transportation, and road repairs, listed for each location. Within each category, the WBS provides a list of particular services, some of them with performance standards. Consistent with performance-based contracting guidance, the contract defines "what" in detail only to the extent needed to communicate the requirement.

For illustrative purposes, Table 2.4 provides a summary of the aggregate WBS that CETAC announced on October 9, 1998, in the RFP. The RFP organizes the WBS by location. Appendix A expands Table 2.4, by including the descriptions of particular services in each category. For example, under "food service operations" in Hungary and Bosnia and Croatia, this version of the WBS calls on the contractor to provide 24-hour food service operation, prepare *three "A" ration meals per day*, utilizing government-furnished foods, and provide limited food service during nonmeal hours. Because needs inevitably change, Table 2.4 and Appendix A are momentary "snapshots," dated October 9, 1998, and are intended to give the reader a feel for the form of the contract.

The contract is a "living" agreement. Despite relatively little change in the broad outline of the WBS, which calls for basic support services, near-continuous updates have addressed changing operational needs with respect to geography and task delineation. For example, the Army modified the list of sites shown in Table 2.4— Home Office, Hungary, and Bosnia and Croatia—almost immediately. CETAC's FY 1999 financial records show charges against task orders for the Home Office—i.e., Houston, Hungary, Bosnia, Albania, Greece, Italy, Macedonia, and Kosovo.[26] A year later, the records show only five sites: Houston, Hungary, Bosnia, Macedonia,

---

[26] Wynn (2000) notes that U.S. forces moved into Kosovo on June 12, 1999.

Table 2.4
Recurring Services in the BSC Request for Proposal

Contractor's Home Office	Hungary	Bosnia and Croatia
Management and administration	Base camp maintenance	Base camp maintenance
Mobilization and demobilization	Laundry service	Laundry service
Freight	Food service operations	Food service operations
Insurance and benefits	Supply service activity operations	Supply service activity operations
	Equipment maintenance	Class III (petroleum supply) operations
	Movements	Equipment maintenance
	Transportation	Movements
	Management and administration	Transportation
	Container-handling services	Road repairs and maintenance
	Shuttle bus services	Management and administration
	Firefighter services	Container-handling services
	Sale of government property	Shuttle bus services
	Hazardous waste management	Mail route operations
	Be prepared for missions	Water services
		Excess property lay-down yard
		Hazardous waste management
		Redeployment staging base area
		Support services to the multinational stabilization forces
		Be prepared for missions

SOURCE: RFP, 1998.
NOTE: For a more detailed presentation, see Appendix A.

and Kosovo. The rapid changes in country composition demonstrate both the dynamism of the operating environment and the flexibility of the contract vehicle.

Obtaining Services

The customer obtains services through task orders. The BSC defines task orders by fiscal year and location. As with the WBSs, they are organized geographically. Each order covers all the services in a particular country—e.g., Hungary.[27] The contractor can perform minor services in another country located near a nation with an established task order, under that task order. If those services take on greater sig-

---

[27] See CETAC (2001b, FAQ 4).

nificance, they may eventually require a separate task order. For example, CETAC describes work in Albania as having been carried out initially under a Macedonia task order but later placed the work under its own task order.[28] Formally, the customer obtains new services in countries with existing task orders, such as Hungary, through a process that ultimately involves modifications or changes to the task order. However, a series of intermediate actions may initiate activities.

The RFP "Special Contract Requirements," p. H-4, section 52.0200-4135, 2(a) and 2(b), depicts the general IDIQ ordering procedures:

> As the needs of the Government are determined, the Contracting Officer (CO) or his authorized representative will notify the contractor of an existing requirement through the issuance of a task order. If a new requirement is received from USAREUR, the contractor shall submit a rough order of magnitude (ROM) to the Administrative Contracting Officer (ACO) in theater, with a copy furnished to the CO. The contractor shall submit their proposal, for accomplishing the new requirement to the CO at the Transatlantic Programs Center.
>
> The proposal is a basis for negotiation of the estimated costs and fees, or negotiation of the costs, depending on what contractual type of task order is issued. The proposal shall provide a detailed breakdown of all items and associated costs anticipated during execution of the Task Order.

Like the contract itself, the order process has evolved over time, responding to changing circumstances and increased concerns about cost. The details of the order process differ, depending on a number of factors, including whether the work is within the scope of the existing agreement, whether it is a one-time assignment or a recurring service, and what it is expected to cost. In general, the degree of oversight grows as the expected cost of the services increases in relation to predetermined cost thresholds—e.g., $1,000, $2,500, and $50,000.

---

[28] See CETAC (2001b, p. 2).

In the next three sections, we describe the formal processes for obtaining services in the BSC. First, we describe the process for service orders—i.e., requests for repairs, maintenance, and other services—relating to existing task orders.[29] Next, we describe the processes for work orders—i.e., orders for new services. New services are either recurring or nonrecurring. Nonrecurring services are also known as unprogrammed new work. We end with a discussion of funds administration.

Service Orders. In the case of a service order, the soldier, unit, or contractor identifies the need or "discrepancy" and reports to the billet office or installation coordinator's office to fill out a service request form.[30] The contractor logs the service order and the installation coordinator (IC) determines if the repair—or other action—is within scope. If it is within scope, the contractor provides the service—e.g. repairs the item.[31] The contractor closes out the log and service request form at the IC's office. At this point, a DCMA quality assurance representative may inspect the log and work and verify completion. If the work passes muster, the service order is closed.

Work Orders. New orders tend to be more complex, usually involving more steps and participants as the anticipated cost rises.[32] Bottom-up requests typically flow from the unit to the IC or project manager; then, if necessary, to other agencies for review and approval; and then, if appropriate, to the ACO for "turn on," pending confirmation of funds. An ACO can activate unprogrammed new work with a notice to proceed (NTP), but only the PCO can turn on

---

[29] CETAC's briefing (2001a) defines a service order as "routine repair and maintenance of existing facilities"—e.g., fixing a leaky faucet. It also defines "new work," which appears to be the residual, as "actions not specifically covered in the Statement of Work." By implication, it would seem that service orders relate to actions that are specifically covered, possibly more than just repairs and maintenance.

[30] The details of this process are drawn from CETAC (2001a). They may have changed slightly since then but remain similar in concept.

[31] If it is not within scope, the service must be requested through the work order process, as outlined below.

[32] This discussion draws heavily from various CETAC documents.

recurring services.[33] All unprogrammed new work is performed on a level of effort (LOE) basis—i.e., with a definitized pot of money for a specified period of time—and the work is folded into an existing task order.[34] LOE funds administration occurs through a "checkbook" process, which is described below. The ACO does not administer funds for recurring services.

The review process depends partly on whether the order is for unprogrammed new work or recurring services and what the order is expected to cost. For unprogrammed new work, the process progresses as follows.

The IC or project manager approves orders valued at less than $1,000 and passes them on to the ACO, who reviews the request and, if it is within scope, issues the NTP, funds pending. The directorate of logistics or DPW chief—within the ASG—approves orders valued from $1,000 to less than $2,500 and passes them on to the ACO for final review and activation.[35] If the cost is expected to reach or exceed $2,500, the ACO initiates another series of steps in a potentially lengthier process that includes JARB validation and source selection, a request for a ROM estimate, and, for orders valued at less than $50,000, TF commander approval.[36] Orders that are expected to cost

---

[33] According to CETAC (2001a), NTPs often contain the words "build," "construct," "install," "erect," or "upgrade." As a legal and financial matter, an NTP gives the contractor the authority to incur costs.

[34] The NTP can and often does precede formal "definitization." As described in the CETAC (1999) statement of procedures for BSC task orders, "Due to the nature of the contract, urgency of the services required and a rapidly changing environment, conventional contracting procedures slow responsiveness, therefore verbal NTPs and RFPs are frequently issued by the PCO. These verbal NTPs and RFPs are followed-up by e-mail confirmation to include funding breakout if applicable and by formal modification at a later date." ACOs can also issue verbal NTPs, in advance of necessary paperwork. According to the CETAC (1999) statement of procedures, "Definitization occurs when a proposal has been received from the contractor, a cost and price analysis has been completed, negotiations are concluded, and a task order or contract modification is issued."

[35] The Contingency Operation Financial Management Implementing Instructions allow procedural discretion for small purchases: "ASG and TF commanders will prescribe local procedures to control approval actions for purchases costing less than $2,500."

[36] A request for a ROM, which is "an unofficial very rough estimate of what it will take for [the contractor] to perform a task force requested project," to be completed by the contractor

$50,000 or more require USAREUR-level approval. As recently as September 2000, the USAREUR approval threshold was set at $100,000—the reduction from $100,000 to $50,000 reflects an increased concern about the cost of the contract.[37]

Figure 2.2 illustrates the order, review, and approval process for unprogrammed new work.[38] For requests originating with the unit, the review and approval process begins with the IC or project manager and flows "up," as required by its expected cost. Though not depicted here, some service requests also originate with USAREUR itself, in which case, a BSC Council of Colonels considers the proposal.

The process is different for recurring services, owing partly to the associated funding stream. USAREUR programs and budgets for recurring work because recurring services imply a continuing need or intent to fund. All recurring service requests, regardless of value, require USAREUR-level approval. Bottom-up requests also involve a JARB review. As noted above, only the PCO can turn on recurring services.

Two questions underlie the order process: is the work necessary and, if it is, who should supply it? As shown in Figure 2.2, the JARB meets to validate the requirement and make a source selection for all new work valued at or above $2,500. As shown in Table 2.5, the JARB's members and advisors typically represent wide-ranging insti-

---

to provide guidance in the decisionmaking process, may also be issued with an NTP. (See CETAC guidance on the use of ROM estimates and CETAC [2001a].) The ROM is developed after TF personnel, the ACO, and the contractor have agreed on the scope of work; moreover, as of March 2000, it can only be requested after the JARB has met and determined that the BSC is the vehicle of choice to execute the work. (See CETAC guidance on use of ROM estimates.) Only the ACO or PCO can request a ROM, because only they can direct work on the contract. (See CETAC, 1999b.) The request for the ROM requires some formality—i.e., an ACO- or PCO-generated NTP—because its preparation entails a reimbursable cost.

[37] CETAC documents dated November 23, 1999, place the threshold at $100,000; GAO (2000a) also places the threshold at $100,000.

[38] This depiction is current as of spring 2003. The source material, a CETAC briefing slide, dated May 6, 2003, includes the caveat, "Major Changes Coming Real Soon."

Figure 2.2
Orders, Reviews, and Approvals for Unprogrammed New Work

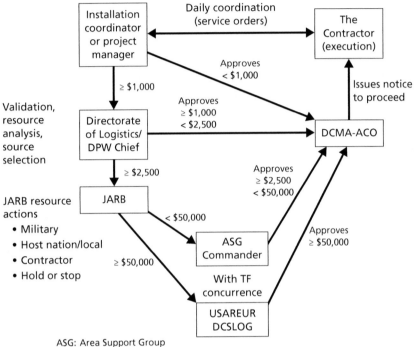

ASG: Area Support Group
DCMA-ACO: Defense Contract Management Agency Administrative Contracting Officer
DPW: Director of Public Works
JARB: Joint Acquisition Review Board
TF: Task Force

SOURCE: CETAC, 2003.
RAND MG282-2.2

tutional perspectives and interests. Members have included representatives of the ASG, G-3 (operations and plans), G-4 (logistics), and
Joint Contracting Center (JCC); advisors have included representatives of the ASG G-1 (personnel), G-6 (signal), DCMA, JCC, and
contractors (USAREUR, 2001). Each member will have a single
voice, and the appropriate approving official will make the final decision. The JCC member and DCMA ACO advisor must be present at
all JARB meetings. The contractor is called in only to answer specific
questions and then is dismissed for the remainder of the meeting.
JARB members should be the primary staff or deputy.

With regard to source selection, the JARB asks who is best suited to provide the service, applying best-value criteria. Options cited in JARB instructions include host nation support, troop labor, local purchase through the JCC, the BSC, USAREUR Engineering Logistics Center, and Army Materiel Command Logistics Support. As noted previously, the Army is not obligated to use the BSC. It can turn to other sources, including other contractors, as it sees fit. Indeed, the JCC sits on the board and can influence sourcing decisions. The JCC reports directly to the USAREUR Contracting Command, which provides USAREUR's Principal Assistant Responsible for Contracting. If other credible contract or noncontract options are under consideration, the selection process can foster competition.

Following JARB validation and source selection, the contractor—e.g., KBR—and customer enter into a period of iterative planning. The contractor submits its plan for filling the order, and the customer bears responsibility for approving, rejecting, or seeking to modify it. Thus, source selection does not imply "free license" for the contractor. The contractor must still meet whatever standards and conditions the customer supplies. During this period, they also negotiate on price and settle on a final cost estimate. This estimate provides the basis for establishing both the base fee and the award fee payments. The ease of this process will likely depend on the extent to which the contractor is drawn into day-to-day planning and operations.

The foregoing discussion reviews formal elements of the order, review, and approval processes that apply to the BSC. However, it does not address the role of the ongoing relationship between the customer and the contractor. Interviews with CETAC, contractors, and others indicate the paramount importance of good communications and give-and-take, both inside and outside the order process. Army doctrine touches on the concept of long-term "habitual relationships" in the context of systems support, but some of the principles may apply here also:

This type of relationship may extend beyond the organization to include the individual contractor employee and soldier. It establishes a comrade-at-arms kinship, which fosters a cooperative harmonious work environment and builds confidence in each other's ability to perform. The existence of a habitual relationship greatly facilitates the planning for predeployment processing, deployment/redeployment, operational and life support, and force protection. (Department of the Army, 2003, p. 2-15.)

With regard to work orders, by all accounts, the sooner the Army brings the contractor into the planning process the better. However, a potential sticking point relates to the treatment of pre-award proprietary cost data. Contractors tend to voice concerns, which the Army echoes in its policy statements, that proprietary information, especially data provided prior to source selection, is treated appropriately and is not used by the Army to "shop around" for better deals.

Funds Administration. Funds typically flow from USAREUR, through CETAC, to the contractor. Historically, CETAC received funds from USAREUR incrementally, throughout the year. However, more recently, transfers have been annualized, also reflecting a change in the overall management of contingency funding (see U.S. GAO, 2002).[39] Starting in FY 2003, USAREUR began programming and budgeting for the funds that pay for the BSC. With occasional exceptions, almost all funding is Operation and Maintenance, Army.[40] Operations and Maintenance, Army, funds are fungible within USAREUR. Funds not committed to the BSC can be spent elsewhere. In practice, USAREUR obligates sufficient funds to the BSC to cover all anticipated costs, including 100 percent of the

---

[39] Under the old incremental system, "The customer, USAREUR [DCS/Logistics], will determine how much funding will be placed on the unprogrammed new-work WBS. The customer will request that the CETAC PCO place these funds on the contract. The PCO will request a proposal from the contractor that breaks down the amount of customer's request." See CETAC (2001b, FAQ 21).

[40] The BSC cannot be used for any permanent military construction; all structures built under the BSC are designed for "temporary use" only. This represents a change in language from the original guidance, which limited spending to temporary structures.

potential award fee. It transfers or "MIPRs" these funds to the U.S. Army Corps of Engineers (USACE) in a lump sum at the beginning of the fiscal year.[41] As of spring 2003, CETAC had enough money committed to fund the BSC through the remainder of FY 2003 at anticipated expenditure rates.

USACE receives and commits funds for task orders. All funding is at the task-order level. As noted previously, the BSC defines task orders by fiscal year and location—e.g., Houston, Hungary, Bosnia, Kosovo, and Macedonia in FY 2003. According to financial records provided in spring 2003, the contract was expected to execute a total of 47 task orders through FY 2004, covering these and other geographic areas. All 47 of the task orders would remain officially open until the final closeout of the contract, to allow adjustments in allowable costs, fee payments, etc. All payments are provisional until the DCAA reviews and verifies them. If KBR does not earn a 100 percent award fee, USACE decommits the unearned amount and retains the funds for use elsewhere on the contract. In principle, USACE can return the funds to USAREUR for use outside the contract, but this has not occurred.

Changes in the contract occur at the level of specific WBS elements, but USACE is free to shift funds within a task order without formally changing the contract.[42] Therefore, it can move money from one previously established WBS element to another as needed, within a task order, to meet theater demands. Geographic additions and deletions notwithstanding, the broad outline of the WBS has changed little since 1999. For example, the Army has added the ASGs and some firefighting services. More often, changes affect the activities within existing WBS elements. Aggregate data on costs by task order and fiscal year are publicly available. Over time, the costs of the contract have declined in aggregate, reflecting the overall level of activity

---

[41] "MIPR" is a verb created from the term, "Military Interdepartmental Purchase Request," referring to the document that formalizes the transfer.

[42] This discussion addresses the process of moving money within task orders, as distinct from the foregoing discussion of the processes required to order new services.

in the region. Figure 2.3 tracks actual and anticipated funding, by location, from 1999 to 2004.

The contractor and PCO track funding for recurring services. The ACOs track funding for unprogrammed new work using a "checkbook."[43] Prior to issuance of a formal task-order modification, the PCO provides the ACOs with a total breakdown of funding that will be added to the task order under unprogrammed new work for tracking by the ACOs in their checkbooks. The breakdown consists of four elements: estimated cost, base fee, potential award fee, and facilities capital cost of money, but the ACO is only responsible for tracking the estimated cost. It is provided to the ACO via e-mail using an Excel spreadsheet formula. Once the spreadsheet data are

Figure 2.3
BSC Funding by Location

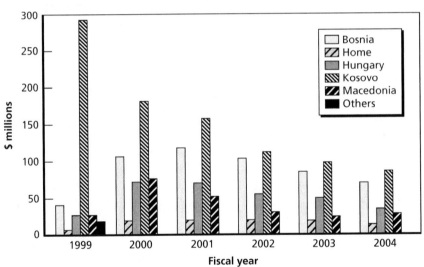

RAND *MG282-2.3*

SOURCE: CETAC financial records, provided May 2003.
NOTE: Figures for 2003 and 2004 are estimates.

---

[43] The following description draws heavily from CETAC (1999b) and from CETAC (2001b). Therefore, some of the terminology, including some of the acronyms, may have changed.

provided, with written direction—in the e-mail—from the PCO requesting the start-up, the ACO can issue an NTP for the unprogrammed new work.[44] A checkbook does not appropriate, obligate, or commit funds; neither is it used to make actual payments. Rather, it is a management device that "controls" funds already committed for use in the BSC. As noted previously, ACOs do not administer funds for recurring services.

The Award Fee and the Evaluation Process

The BSC establishes an "award fee pool" equal to 8 percent of the negotiated *estimated* cost for each review period, set at four-month intervals. The Award Fee Determining Official (AFDO) awards some or all of the pool, depending on the contractor's performance during the review period. Whereas the 1 percent base fee is automatic, the payment of any award fee is contingent on the contractor exceeding a minimum overall rating.[45] The overall rating is the weighted average of numeric scores in three functional areas: funds management and cost control; performance; and coordination, flexibility, and responsiveness. An unearned award fee from one review period does not carry over to subsequent periods.

The RFP outlines a four-step hierarchical award fee evaluation process, which has remained largely unchanged over the past several years:

---

[44] More precisely, the message includes the amount of estimated cost, which establishes the "checkbook" balance from which the ACO can issue NTPs.

[45] Because the base fee is automatic and is set as a share of the negotiated estimated—not actual—cost, it is essentially fixed. Similarly, the upper bound on the award fee is also fixed. Thus, the contractor has no incentive after the negotiation to incur higher costs to get more fees. However, it may have some incentive to produce a higher-than-necessary cost estimate at the outset. This implies that the Army must carefully evaluate cost estimates and consider—e.g., through the JARB process—the possibility of using other service providers for new work requirements to encourage competition.

- The contractor's performance is evaluated and monitored by performance evaluators (PEs).[46]
- The PEs submit evaluations, with qualitative and quantitative ratings based on stated award fee evaluation criteria, to the Award Fee Evaluation Board (AFEB).
- The AFEB evaluates the contractor's performance and the AFEB chairman submits the findings to the AFDO.[47] The AFEB performs the evaluation by reviewing
  — the contractor's performance, measured against the award fee evaluation criteria, and
  — the contractor's written documentation or oral presentation describing their performance for the period.[48]
- The AFDO may accept the findings or award a fee as he or she determines. The decision of the AFDO is final.[49]

For each period, the Award Fee Determining Plan (AFDP) establishes the procedures for the determination of contractor performance and the award fee payable to the contractor.[50] The plan also specifies the appointment of the AFDO, the membership of the AFEB, and the origination of the PEs:

- The Corp of Engineers Principal Assistant Responsible for Contracting appoints the AFDO in writing.

---

[46] CETAC (2002c, p. 3) notes that PEs also bear responsibility for providing "continuous evaluation" of contractor performance in their assigned area. The amount of oversight is up to each PE, but "daily oversight is the foundation of the award fee evaluation process."

[47] The AFEB meets in Germany for one day, every four months, to conduct the review.

[48] According to the September 2002 AFDP, the AFEB may invite the PEs and the contractor to make presentations to the board relative to performance during the evaluation period.

[49] The decision of the AFDO and the award fee payment are not subject to the contract's "Disputes" and "Limitation of Funds" clauses, respectively.

[50] It supplies the detail for implementing the evaluation process under the contract, serving as a charter for the organizational structure required to direct and execute the contract award fee clauses; identifying the functional performance areas, evaluation criteria, and rating plan for monitoring, assessing and evaluating contractor performance; and providing a consistent method for the equitable and timely determination of an award fee earned. See CETAC (2002a).

- The AFEB consists of, but is not limited to, the following members, of which the first nine are voting members and the last three are nonvoting, advisory members:
  — AFEB Chairman, as appointed by the AFDO[51]
  — USAREUR Deputy Chief of Staff (DCS)/Logistics representative
  — USAREUR DCS/Engineering representative
  — USAREUR DCS/Resource Management representative
  — USAREUR DCS/Personnel and Installations Management representative
  — DCMA representative
  — DCMA representative
  — CETAC representative
  — CETAC representative
  — CETAC BSC project team members, as required
  — CETAC legal counsel
  — CETAC recorder.
- PEs "shall" include the PCO and all ACOs as well as a DCAA representative; the PEs should include, but are not limited to, DCMA-SE (Defense Contract Management Agency–Southern Europe) CCAS (Contingency Contract Administration Services) commanders, ASG commander with selected members of his or her staff, and staffs of the supporting task force.

The RFP sets out award fee evaluation criteria for each of three functional areas and a formula for calculating an overall score. The areas—funds management and cost control; performance; and coordination, flexibility, and responsiveness—have not changed over the life of the contract, but the criteria and rating formula have. We highlight some significant differences in the criterian and rating formula in the RFP and a more recent AFDP below.

---

[51] Per the September 19, 2002, AFDP, p. 3, "The AFEB Chairman will normally be the CETAC Director of Engineering and Construction Management."

In accordance with the September 2002 AFDP, the PEs score the contractor as either outstanding, 95–100 points; excellent, 91–94 points; very good, 81–90 points; good, 71–80 points; satisfactory, 61–70 points; and poor or unsatisfactory, less than 61 points. In the RFP, only three ratings brackets can be found: above average, 71–100 points; average, 61–70 points; and below average, 0–60 points. The change affords the evaluators less discretion in the award process and may serve to raise the bar for the contractor, particularly in conjunction with other changes in weights and evaluation criteria (see discussion below and later with Figure 3.7).

The ratings for each area are weighted to arrive at an overall, or "total weighted rating," for the period. In the September 2002 AFDP, the funds management and cost control area accounts for 40 percent of the aggregate; the performance area accounts for 30 percent; and the coordination, flexibility, and responsiveness area accounts for another 30 percent. In contrast, the weights in the RFP were set at 30 percent, 35 percent, and 35 percent, respectively.

The contractor receives a percentage of the award fee pool, calculated as 8 percent of the estimated cost for the review period, according to the schedule shown in Figure 2.4.

A comparison of the RFP and the AFDP indicates a significant change in emphasis over time, at least some of which may have been responses to concerns raised in a GAO report.[52] Cost, especially cost *reduction*, has gained prominence, both quantitatively and qualitatively. Perhaps the most obvious change, "funds management and cost control," accounts for 40 percent of the contractor's overall evaluation score, up from 30 percent in the RFP. Qualitatively, the emphasis has shifted from staying within projections—a top score previously required few if any negative surprises—to reducing costs. Initially, the first line of the cost criteria reads, "all projections are met." Only midway through did the criteria seek savings, "continuing efforts are made to reduce costs with a high degree of success." The

---

[52] We discuss the relationship between GAO's comments on cost and changes in Army practices later in this report.

Figure 2.4
Award Fee Schedule

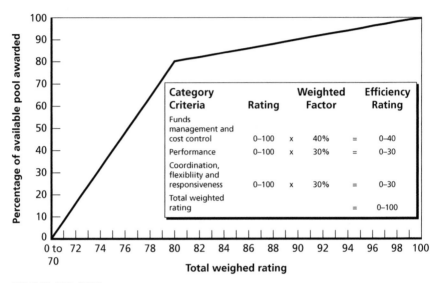

SOURCE: RFP; 2002 memo.
RAND *MG282-2.4*

NOTE: The weighting factors for funds management, performance, and coordination were set at 30, 35, and 35 percent, respectively, in the RFP, but were revised to 40, 30, and 30 percent in 2002.

AFDP refers to accurate projections first, but turns immediately to economies and cost reduction, "It [the cost area] also includes economies in the use of personnel, energy, materials, facilities and transportation. Cost reductions may be achieved through new initiatives that save government resources, the use of cost savings programs, [or the use of] cost avoidance programs."

Moreover, for a top evaluation score, the AFDP now requires continuous improvements. The contractor must show new additional cost savings in each review period to receive an "outstanding" rating: "Performance is outstanding in all significant aspects and improved measurably over the period under consideration. New initiatives which measurably improved efficiency and saved the government resources were implemented during this rating period."

In a later discussion of the BSC track record, we report the contractor's scores from November 1999 to March 2003. Differences in scores before and after the changes in brackets, weights, and criteria took effect may provide some insight to their net effect, but it is difficult to attribute the differences to any particular change because they were all introduced at the same time in 2002.

The Contract Data Requirements List and Other Tools

The CDRL consists of a set of more than 20 data requirements, with reports varying in frequency from daily—i.e., the situation report—to "as needed." Through the CDRL reports, the contractor provides information on nearly every aspect of the contract's operation, covering such more or less predictable topics as travel, lessons learned, the cost of work, the day's events, cost avoidance measures, the number of contractor personnel in theater, construction, other-than-trash found in dumpsters, and pesticide applications.[53]

The CDRL reports are widely distributed to CETAC, USAREUR, DCMA, DCAA, the base camps, and other sites. With these data, the Army can track nearly any variable of interest. Thus, the CDRL reports offer a potentially powerful management and oversight tool.

The BSC contains several other "built-in" management and oversight tools. A CETAC briefing lists various "controls over contractor." In addition to the award fee process and CDRL reports, it includes the "Limitation of Funds" and "Limitation of Costs" letters, noting that if there is no money the contractor "goes home." It includes the contractor's Quality Control and Quality Assurance Plan. It also lists several items that relate to the work order process but are not necessarily built into the contract explicitly—e.g., CETAC pricing evaluations, CETAC task order spreadsheets, BCCA (more recently the ASGs) roles and functions, and JARB "Contingency Operations Financial Management Implementation Instructions."

---

[53] CETAC provided the CDRL report description and the report distribution list.

These last several items suggest ways in which the work order process is, in and of itself, a built-in management and oversight tool. Although not always framed as such, it provides a key opportunity to manage and oversee the contract. Each new order offers an occasion to reevaluate the contractor by asking who is best suited to provide the service. Although JARB evaluations are tied directly to the contractor's desirability in providing a particular new service, the process implicitly raises the question, "Is the Army satisfied with the contractor's performance?"

Summary and Observations

The preplanned, performance-based IDIQ, CPAF formulation of the BSC may obviate the need for micromanagement, but it does not obviate the need for management entirely. The contract's built-in management and oversight tools, including performance evaluation and work order processes, provide avenues for governance, but they require effective use, which, in turn, requires effective coordination. The Army's discussion of "habitual relationships" also suggests the importance of cohesion.

The large number of DoD agencies with management or oversight roles presents opportunities and challenges, particularly with respect to coordination. These participants are institutionally varied and geographically diffuse, operating in the United States, Germany, and the Balkans. They convey a valuable diversity of perspectives. The BSC uses a variety of institutional structures to draw them together, including the ASGs, JARB, and AFEB.[54] Regularly scheduled JARB and AFEB meetings provide other venues for coordination. They may also serve coordinating functions beyond their defined roles in acquisitions and performance evaluations, merely by bringing many participants together in one place at one time.

---

[54] Some if not all BCCA functions have been rolled into the ASGs.

Coordination, however, is not limited to DoD agencies and their personnel. It must also involve the contractor and its BSC-dedicated employees, some of whom are located in the United States. Previously, the BCCA filled a coordinating function aimed at drawing the customer and contractor together and potentially encouraging cohesion through training, townhall meetings, etc. Whether the new ASG's fill this role—or need to fill this role—is unclear.[55] On the one hand, the contract may have matured sufficiently to no longer require such formal mechanisms. That is, the customer and contractor may have established something akin to a habitual relationship, promoting coordination and cohesion—absent more bureaucratic means. On the other hand, given the steady flow of Army personnel and contracting officials through the area of operation, more formal efforts may still be needed.

The steady flow of personnel also speaks to the need for adequate training. Institutions alone are not enough to ensure coordination or cohesion. Personnel must have the know-how to put them to use. This may be especially challenging in a dynamic environment. The adequacy of training—and institutional memory—has attracted attention in previous reports. For ACOs and other administrative field staff, GAO (2000a) comments on problems of short tours—routinely six months.[56] In response, DCMA began scheduling tours with three-month overlaps, to help smooth staffing transitions and improve learning. Moreover, GAO and others have made the case that ACOs often lack experience with this type of contract. By some accounts, the pool of qualified candidates may even also be shrinking. Adding to the concern, field staff may be receiving less training than

---

[55] The JARB and AFEB may serve integrative functions vis-á-vis the contractor, but they are not necessarily cohesion-promoting institutions. They do not encourage a two-way flow of information or ideas in planning or executing operations, except insofar as the AFEB allows or requires the contractor to contribute to its meeting. One opportunity for feedback appears to be lacking. When asked, CETAC seemed to indicate that, after the evaluation is complete, the AFEB does not provide the contractor with specific information on the areas of its performance requiring improvement.

[56] GAO (2003) provides further comments on training adequacy.

they once did. Additional training for end users may also be necessary to enable them to get the most out of the contract.

Each of these issues suggests a possible source of risk. We address each of them in the following chapters in the contexts of risk management, residual risks, review processes, and lessons learned.

CHAPTER THREE

Risk Management in Theory and Practice

The recently revised Army field manual, *Contractors on the Battlefield*, calls for risk management in planning and implementing contracts to provide CSS.[1] Army and joint doctrine, presented in two other publications—both of which are aptly titled *Risk Management*—provides practical guidance. Application of the doctrine requires systematic consideration of what can go wrong in an operation, contract, or other military environment, including the potential severity of the consequences. It can also facilitate priority-setting for risk mitigation.

In this chapter, we present the risk-management doctrine and apply it to the BSC and its operating environment. First, we review basic risk-related vocabulary. Then, we present a methodology for identifying, assessing, and controlling risk, which derives almost entirely from Army and joint doctrine. Although geared toward operational considerations, the approach is intended for—and appropriate to—wider use. Next, we provide examples relevant to the BSC to illustrate the basic principles of risk management and to identify some of the underlying sources of risk in the BSC and its operating environment. In view of this methodology, we discuss the approaches that the Army has taken to manage risks in the BSC specifically and the results of those efforts.

---

[1] See discussion in Department of the Army (2003), Chapter One, under "Governing Principles of Contractor Support," p. 1-8, and in Chapter Two, under "Risk Assessment," pp. 2-8 and 2-9.

What Is Risk?

We start by reviewing basic definitions from the Army and other military references. The Army defines *risk* as the "chance of hazard or bad consequences; the probability of exposure to chance of injury or loss from a hazard; risk level is expressed in terms of hazard probability and severity" (Department of the Army, 1998b, p. Glossary-2). As such, risk involves two key components, the "chance" and the "hazard." The Army further defines *hazard* as "a condition or activity with potential to cause damage, loss, or mission degradation" and any actual or potential condition that can cause

- injury, illness, or death of personnel;
- damage to or loss of equipment and property; or
- mission degradation (Department of the Army, 1998b, pp. Glossary-1 and 2-2).[2]

Army doctrine emphasizes operational factors but is explicitly intended for wider use. From Department of the Army (1998b, p. ii), "Although the manual's prime focus is on the operational Army, the principles of risk management apply to all Army activities." Department of the Army (1998b, p. 1-4) asserts "risk management applies to all situations and environments across a wide range of Army operations, activities, and processes" and "is useful in developing, fielding, and employing the total Army force."

The approach taken in joint doctrine is generally consistent with that taken in the Army doctrine, with only minor differences in vocabulary and focus. For example, the joint doctrine refers to "threats," not "hazards" (Department of the Army et al., 2001, p. Glossary-6). The 2001 Quadrennial Defense Review Report calls attention to an even wider range of hazards, threats, or bad consequences, relating to

---

[2] Department of the Army (1998b, p. ii) defines the term "mission" as including "mission, operation, or task."

- force management, the ability to recruit, retain, and equip sufficient numbers of quality personnel and sustain the readiness of the force while accomplishing its many operational tasks;
- operations, the ability to achieve military objectives in a near-term conflict or other contingency;
- future challenges, the ability to invest in new capabilities and develop new operational concepts needed to dissuade or defeat mid- to long-term military challenges; and
- institutions, the ability to develop management practices and controls that use resources efficiently and promote the effective operation of the defense establishment (DoD, 2001, pp. 57–65).

Drawing from each of these sources, we take a broad view of "downside" risk in considering potential hazards across wide-ranging military activities and objectives.[3] Although generally consistent with the doctrine, we elaborate further by dividing potential hazards, hence risk, into two categories of our own design. One category involves the performance of particular services or activities, such as those listed in the BSC's WBS. We define performance to include quality (a service may be performed inadequately or, in the extreme, not at all) and cost. The other category involves "higher-order" concerns, including mission success, force management, and security. We define security as the safety of military and nonmilitary personnel (including contractor employees), property, and information. The two categories may be interrelated—that is, a problem arising in the performance of an individual activity could affect mission success, force management or security, and, in some instances, vice versa.

In the next section, we introduce a methodology for identifying, assessing, and controlling risk. It draws directly from a combination

---

[3] We do not, however, take the broadest possible view of risk. In this discussion, we focus on undesirable outcomes—e.g., unexpectedly low quality or high costs—but risk is not one-sided. Outcomes may be better than expected—quality may be higher or costs may be lower than anticipated. Indeed, to exploit the opportunities of "upside" risk, one may be forced to tolerate some of the "downside." As a corollary, by seeking to mitigate the downside, one might expunge the upside.

of Army and joint doctrine. We use it as a basis for discussing the types of activity and higher-order hazards relevant to the BSC and for addressing their causality. Both the doctrine and our analysis suggest the importance of establishing causality, particularly *underlying* or *root* causality. Absent a clear understanding of the source of a particular risk, the Army stands to choose an inappropriate control and potentially weaken its position.

Practical Guidance for Managing Risk

This section reviews the basic approach to risk management presented in Army and joint doctrine. The doctrine tends to be operationally oriented, but the basic framework can be applied to all Army activities, including contracting. As shown in Figure 3.1, Army and joint doctrine outline a five-step continuous risk management process.[4] It begins with a mission but could begin with a make-or-buy decision; the design of a new acquisition strategy, source-selection process, or contract; or the call for new activities under an existing contract. We focus on potential contracting applications.

Steps one and two constitute "risk assessment," including identification; steps three to five are the "essential follow-through actions to effectively manage risk" (Department of the Army, 1998b, p. 2-2). We refer to the last three steps collectively as "risk mitigation." Step three sets out the initial risk controls; the last two steps generate experience and feedback, which can result in a change of course or a procedural refinement, as needed. These final steps can result in changes within or to the contract's operating mechanisms, but lessons learned can also yield changes in broader policy at higher levels.

---

[4] Department of the Army et al. (2001) provides a consolidated multiservice reference. It explains the risk management process and highlights differences and similarities as each service applies it. For the most part, this joint publication repeats the same five-step framework found in Department of the Army (1998b). Where interesting differences arise, we note them below.

Figure 3.1
Five-Step Risk Management Process

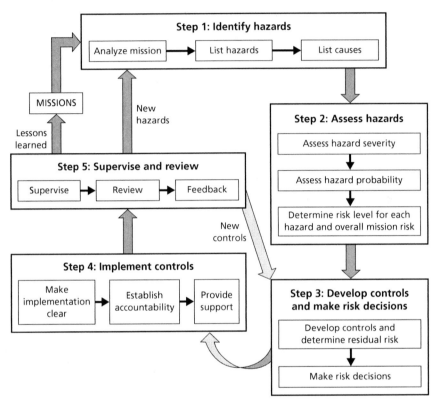

SOURCES: Department of the Army (1998b); Department of the Army et al. (2001).

RAND MG282-3.1

NOTE: Department of the Army et al. (2001) refers to "threats," whereas Department of the Army (1998b) refers to "hazards." In this figure, we use the word "hazard." Department of the Army et al. (2001) also articulates several substeps, such as "list causes," that are not articulated in Department of the Army (1998b); we include them in this figure.

Department of the Army et al. (2001, p. II-1) stresses the "paramount" importance of determining the root cause or causes of each hazard to improve the effectiveness of risk controls. Although Department of the Army (1998b) does not address this point, we believe that establishing causality is essential. Absent a clear understanding of causality, the Army stands to choose the wrong control, which, at the very least, would be less effective than it otherwise could be, potentially leaving the Army vulnerable to the hazard it initially uncovered in step one. Choosing the wrong control could also weaken an otherwise strong process or operation, creating a new vulnerability or causing additional harm. A series of examples demonstrates this point in the following section.

Ideally, step two would include estimation of both the probability and severity of a potential loss. Both Army and joint doctrine provide a measurement tool. This tool, which takes the form of a matrix, facilitates the systematic evaluation of risks and priorities (see Figure 3.2). Quantitative data can be used to inform the evaluation, but the matrix does not fundamentally require quantification. Rather, it requires expert opinion. As described in Department of the Army et

Figure 3.2
Risk Assessment Matrix: Assessing Severity and Probability

Severity		Probability				
		Frequent A	Likely B	Occasional C	Seldom D	Unlikely E
Catastrophic	I	E	E	H	H	M
Critical	II	E	H	H	M	L
Marginal	III	H	M	M	L	L
Negligible	IV	M	L	L	L	L

E Extremely high risk   H High risk   M Moderate risk   L Low risk

SOURCES: Department of the Army (1998b); Department of the Army et al. (2001).
RAND MG282-3.2

al. (2001, p. A-D-1), "The Risk Assessment Matrix combines severity and probability estimates to form a risk assessment for each threat [hazard]." It can be used "to evaluate the acceptability of a risk and the level at which the decision on acceptability will be made. The matrix may also be used to prioritize resources, to resolve risks, or to standardize threat notification or response actions." Department of the Army et al. (2001, p. II-2) explicitly cites prioritization as an output of risk assessment. Combined with other information about expected costs, of both the risk and mitigation, the process can help the Army determine which risks it should address and how.

Risk control, which occurs in steps three, four, and five as part of risk mitigation, would involve developing a strategy for eliminating, reducing, or coping with the possibility of a hazard. By implication, the goal of risk mitigation is not necessarily risk elimination. In some instances, it may be preferable to accept some amount of "residual risk" and develop a response and recovery plan. Although not shown in Figure 3.1, step three, "Develop and Make Risk Decisions," also requires evaluation of controls for suitability, feasibility, and acceptability, where acceptability refers, in part, to cost-benefit assessment (see Department of the Army, 1998b, p. 2-14).

According to the doctrine, risk management should occur explicitly and continuously from the first phases of planning through the final phases of execution. The Army's first principle of risk management is "integrating risk management into mission planning, preparation, and execution" (Department of the Army, 1998b, p. 1-3). Later, we review the methods of risk assessment and mitigation that the Army has employed in planning and implementing the BSC and compare them with the doctrinal ideal.

Applying Risk Management Principles to the BSC

Having reviewed the general definitions and methodologies, we now apply them in the context of the BSC. First, we identify and discuss potential hazards; second, we address causality, demonstrating an approach to determining root or underlying causes, known as a "fault tree" analysis. As we discuss, assessing probability and severity proves more challenging.

Identifying Potential Hazards

Close consideration of the BSC and its operating environment suggests dividing potential hazards, hence risk, into two categories: one involving the performance of a particular service or activity and the other involving higher-order concerns, such as mission success, force management, and security. However, significant relationships and trade-offs may exist both within and across categories. Here, we address these types of potential hazards in relation to the BSC. In so doing, we also demonstrate the difficulty of listing hazards without addressing causality.

Activity-Related Hazards. The performance of every item listed in the contract's WBS entails at least two kinds of potential hazards: one relates to quality, including nonperformance, and the other to cost. Consider these hazards in the context of BSC food service operations. The WBS calls for 24-hour service, consisting of three "A" ration meals and limited non–meal hour service. In this case, the service could be inadequate, possibly unperformed, or too costly. But what do "inadequate" or "too costly" mean? We pose two additional questions for rhetorical purposes: does the contractor provide the *requested* services, and do those services cost more than they *should?*

The "request" in the first question draws attention to the participation of both the customer and the contractor. If all goes well, the customer places an order, the contractor fills it, and both parties are satisfied. However, opportunities for disappointment exist on both sides. From the customer's perspective, it may not get what it asked for or it may get what it asked for, only to discover that it asked for the wrong thing.

To "not get what it asked for" can range from a minor deficiency to complete nonperformance—e.g., the difference between mediocre food and no food. As we discuss below, the failure may or may not be the contractor's fault. To have "asked for the wrong thing" speaks to a different, but equally important, aspect of the contracting relationship: the customer cannot reasonably expect to get something other than the service it requests. By implication, it must know when and how to place the *right* order. The need for a well-formulated request may seem trivial and obvious, but it may lie at the heart of some apparent but misperceived contract failures.

In the second question, the word "should" raises the possibility of at least two problems with cost. One relates to expectations: do actual costs exceed projected costs? The other problem relates to cost-effectiveness: are the cost to the government, either actual or expected, low enough, for a given level of quality? The first type of hazard is relatively straightforward. The government can compare actual costs to expected or budgeted costs. The second is more challenging. Whether costs meet or exceed expectations may provide little insight to whether the cost is low enough.

Quality and cost are often interrelated, typically through a very direct mechanism. As a practical matter, a service provider, be it a contract provider or any other type of provider, can almost always offer more or better service, potentially eliciting a higher degree of customer satisfaction, if they spend more. Whether, or to what extent, a provider chooses to "gold plate" a service would likely depend on the terms of the contract, memorandum of understanding (MOU), operational plan, or other guidance. We address this issue later in the context of causality.

In the simplest possible terms, we could draw a list of activity-related hazards directly from the WBS in Appendix A. For each service, there is a chance that it will be underperformed with respect to either quality or cost—or possibly both. However, a WBS-derived laundry list of hazards absent any further analysis would be of little practical value. It is simply a starting point for systematically identifying concerns. Clearly, myriad things can go wrong for myriad reasons. Some failures are more likely than others, with effects ranging from "negligible" to "catastrophic." This creates a need to explore the underlying causality, probability, and severity to arrive at the right mitigation strategy and control mechanisms.

Hazards Relating to Higher-Order Concerns. Higher-order concerns involve mission success, force management, and security of personnel, property, and information. Examples of hazards include failures to serve peacekeeping functions, difficulty recruiting and retaining troops, death or serious injury of military or civilian personnel, loss of essential equipment, and intelligence leaks. They can also be interrelated, though not necessarily involving the kinds of direct trade-offs addressed in the context of quality and cost. Indeed, some hazards are reinforcing—e.g., an intelligence breach may endanger military and nonmilitary personnel and jeopardize peacekeeping objectives.

Here too, clarifying the interrelatedness of hazards leads quickly to a discussion of causality. A higher-order hazard may involve the performance of a specific activity or it may involve more general circumstances. To illustrate, consider the possibility of a contract employee's injury. A contract employee may be at risk of injury because of the nature of the particular activity that he or she is undertaking—for example, handling volatile chemical substances or other hazardous materials. Or the employee may be at risk because of general deficiencies in planning and coordination processes—for example, the Army may not have planned for the resources needed to protect contract employees in a hostile work environment.[5]

Examples of activity-derived higher-order hazards abound, ranging from the dramatic to the mundane. The WBS calls for the contractor to deliver potable water for drinking, kitchens, showers, and other uses. The associated activity hazards include too little water at too high cost—but, possibly of even greater concern, they also include the inadvertent or intentional provision of contaminated water. At the very least, a contaminated water supply could cause minor discomfort, but, if it resulted in widespread and severe illness, it could hamper the mission. Less dramatic failures can also take their toll. Mediocre food, dirty laundry, and soiled living quarters can

---

[5] Referring to LOGCAP, "A salient contract condition is that contractor personnel are provided security by the deployed U.S. forces. While this appears to be a simple provision, it has proven difficult to execute, especially at the beginning and end of events. Therefore, the operational commander now has an additional security requirement to consider in his planning" (Kolar, 1997).

affect troops' morale, which can eventually hurt recruiting and retention.

In some cases, the linkages within and across categories are more complex, involving multiple layers of feedback—e.g., from security to mission success, from security to service delivery, and from service delivery back to mission success. Returning to the force protection example, the Army may need to provide extra troops to protect contract employees, but it may also need to draw resources from other core functions to do so, potentially jeopardizing the success of the mission, particularly if the need is unanticipated. Moreover, some protective measures, such as ID checks and roadblocks, may interfere with the contractor's ability to provide timely delivery, transportation, or other services, thereby reducing their quality or raising their cost. Slow deliveries of essential goods, such as fuel, could also impair the mission.

As with activity-level hazards, things can go wrong in countless ways and for countless reasons. Understanding how different types of hazards are interrelated is an essential part of understanding why bad things happen and, ultimately, how to either keep them from happening or respond and recover when they do happen. The importance of understanding different hazards', hence risks', interrelatedness in formulating appropriate strategies and controls will become more apparent as we delve into causality.

Mapping Hazards to Root Causes

The WBS provides a practical starting point for tracing causality, especially with respect to activity-related hazards. For each element in the WBS, we can identify potential hazards and consider possible proximate and root causes. A single hazard could spring from more than one event. For example, an episode of water contamination could result from human error, a mechanical failure, or intentional interference, among other things. As in the case of quality and cost, one hazard might relate to another. To untangle the sources of higher-order hazards, we can ask whether they can be traced to particular WBS elements or general conditions in the operating environment.

Somewhat more formally, we can undertake a simplified form of "fault tree" analysis, in which we start at the "top" with a particular negative outcome and seek its underlying cause or causes. This methodology applies equally well to activity-related and higher-order hazards. Ideally, we would estimate the probability of the outcome by tracing the likelihood of each element in the casual chain. Thus the tree would embody elements of threat identification and assessment and draw together many of the principles addressed in Army and joint doctrine—specifically, those found in steps one and two of the five-step risk-management process.

Alternatively, we could invert the analytical technique and start from the "bottom," with potential causes and ask what negative outcomes they might lead to. In the foregoing discussion of water contamination leading to illness and mission impairment, we took a bottom-up approach. In so doing, we also demonstrated an important aspect of risk analysis: a negative outcome at one level could be the cause of a negative outcome at another level. Perspective may define cause and effect.

In this section, we present a series of hypothetical fault trees to illustrate both the methodology and some of the causal issues raised in the previous section. The examples are synthetic, in that they are drawn from activities listed in the WBS, from the operating environment, or from unconfirmed anecdote, but they are not intentionally derived from any documented incidents or complaints. They are intended to be realistic only to the extent that they or some variants could plausibly occur or have occurred given the contents of the WBS and the nature of the operating environment. Taking a top-down approach, we posit a particular negative outcome and trace its origins to a particular event or incentive—the underlying or root cause. Through these examples, we illustrate how apparent failures can arise from "getting what you ask for," trading quality for cost, and planning and coordination problems, though not necessarily from the decision to contract, per se. However, we do not attempt to assess the probability of the posited outcome or of any of the causal factors leading to them.

As the analytical process unfolds, it becomes even more apparent that root causes can be elusive. One can almost always peel back another layer of causality or search further back into the origin of an event, leading finally to a cause far beyond practical or useful reach. In these illustrative scenarios, we limit the analysis to possible causes within the jurisdiction of the BSC and the planning and coordination processes that can or should directly support the larger operation. Among the latter, we include those responsible for integrating the BSC with other contract and noncontract activities. Other potentially relevant processes include those supporting the initial or recurring make-or-buy decisions and source selections, including reopening competition.

Figure 3.3 illustrates the basic approach for a generic performance failure, such as the failure to deliver fuel where or when it was needed. We start by tracing the failure to its proximate cause or

Figure 3.3
The Proximate Causes of a Generic Performance Failure

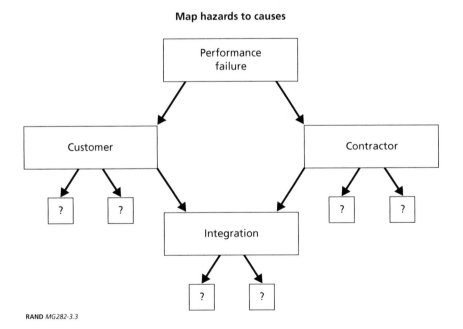

causes, possibly a customer- or contractor-based problem, and then drill down to the root cause or causes, noting that some shortcomings, such as those relating to integration, can cause customer or contractor failures.

The tree in Figure 3.3 has two main root systems, or paths, starting with either an apparent customer or contractor failure. For example, the customer may have placed the order for the fuel delivery too late or the contractor may have been unprepared to fill it, lacking a truck, a driver, or the fuel. Drilling further down, we find that problems relating to integration can generate what appear to be customer or contractor failures, sometimes providing a direct link between the two. For example, the customer may have been responsible, under the terms of the contract, for purchasing the fuel but failed to make timely payment, thereby delaying the shipment past its due date.

As the next three examples also show, merely identifying a proximate cause is not necessarily enough to arrive at an appropriate management strategy. In each case, we drill down from the proximate cause to the root cause, asking "why" or "why not" at each juncture and revealing the inadequacy of a proximate inspection. We do not explore every imaginable cause but focus on particular paths to make specific points about the methodology, its application, and causality.

Figure 3.4 illustrates an apparent service deficiency. What if hot meals are not available 24 hours a day, seven days a week? When this failure occurs, the proximate cause is understaffing. However, a closer look at the WBS reveals a poorly framed request—the customer got what it asked for, "limited service during nonmeal hours," but asked for the wrong thing. Or it intentionally asked for a lesser service at the outset, in view of competing demands, but later regretted the decision. If the analysis had stopped at the proximate cause—i.e., understaffing—we would almost certainly have recommended the wrong risk controls, perhaps trying to alter the contract to mandate minimum staffing levels during nonmeal hours.

This example also illustrates some ways in which a risk may or may not arise from the sourcing decision. The issue of determining

**Figure 3.4
"You Get What You Ask For"**

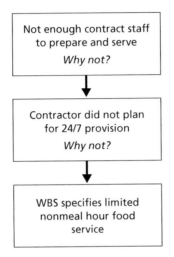

What if hot meals are not available 24/7?

Not enough contract staff
to prepare and serve
Why not?

↓

Contractor did not plan
for 24/7 provision
Why not?

↓

WBS specifies limited
nonmeal hour food
service

NOTE: This example draws from an unconfirmed anecdote raised early in the project. Army staff mentioned possible concerns about a lack of hot meal service during off hours.
RAND *MG282-3.4*

requirements is independent of the type of source. An inadequately framed request or a change in the customer's needs is not a purely "contractual" problem. It could occur under any service-providing arrangement, be it a CSS contract, MOU, or otherwise. Two important questions here are how quickly and at what cost the provider can meet the customer's needs, once it has established and asserted them, and how do alternative providers compare on this basis? If an arrangement is flexible and responsive, whatever its form, a deficiency can be remedied. We have no clear a priori basis for asserting that an organic service provider would be able to respond to a restatement of requirements more quickly than a contractor or at lower cost.

Figure 3.5 illustrates the relationship between contract incentives and cost risk, highlighting the roles of both the contractor and

Figure 3.5
Incentives and Quality-Cost Trade-Offs

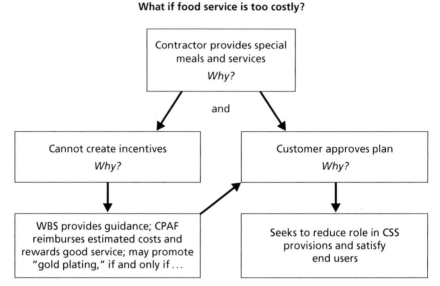

What if food service is too costly?

Contractor provides special
meals and services
Why?

and

Cannot create incentives
Why?

Customer approves plan
Why?

WBS provides guidance; CPAF
reimburses estimated costs and
rewards good service; may promote
"gold plating," if and only if ...

Seeks to reduce role in CSS
provisions and satisfy
end users

NOTE: This example draws on the CPAF evaluation criteria in the RFP; more recent
descriptions of the criteria have sought to place greater emphasis on cost reductions
and efficiency.
RAND *MG282-3.5*

the customer in eliciting "too costly" performance. The contract
might create incentives to overserve and overspend, but this can only
happen with the customer's approval. However, if the customer seeks
to reduce its role in CSS provision, it might choose this route to
ensure end-user satisfaction. In this example, the customer got what it
asked for, and quite possibly what it wanted, but had to pay for it.

As in Figure 3.4, the apparent failure is not necessarily a contract
failure. Depending on the balance of the Army's objectives, the
incentive to overserve and overspend, commonly referred to as "gold
plating," might prevail, regardless of the sourcing decision. If, as
above, end-user satisfaction is a top priority, the Army might choose a
higher level of service, at higher cost, even if it fills the requirement
with military personnel. The trade-off between quality and cost may

arise no matter who serves the food or, more generally, provides the service.

The BSC presents opportunities to reduce the risk of over-spending through existing management and oversight mechanisms, including performance evaluations and reviews, but a solution might require either more self-discipline on the part of the customer or an open admission of its willingness to incur higher costs for better or added service. If the customer knows that it cannot exercise self-discipline in the moment, during operations, it could also choose to tie its hands at the outset by making its demands more explicit in the WBS. However, this approach could entail other costs, including a loss of flexibility (which could limit the contractor's ability to respond to new opportunities and needs) and the additional requirement for day-to-day management of a more specific tasking. Of course, the ultimate solution need not be all or nothing but might involve a balance of these approaches.

Figure 3.6 illustrates the mapping process for a higher-order hazard that does not track neatly to a specific WBS activity but relates more generally to problems of planning, coordination, and integration. In this scenario, contract personnel are injured because military personnel are not available to protect them. Why not? Because the customer did not plan for the security requirement. Why not? Because the customer was not aware of its responsibility or, possibly, because its responsibility was ambiguous. The ambiguity may arise directly from the operating environment. For example, criminal activities may pose dangers not envisioned at the start of the operation. A truck might be waylaid en route, say, not by enemy fire but by thieves. Visibility may be another factor. The customer might be aware of its responsibilities but might not know the whereabouts of those for whom it is responsible.

In this case, addressing the proximate cause—e.g., by shifting military personnel to provide protection—might be the only immediate answer but would not constitute a solution. A solution should address the underlying planning and coordination failures, otherwise it might unleash other problems. For example, shifting resources

Figure 3.6
Planning or Coordination Failures

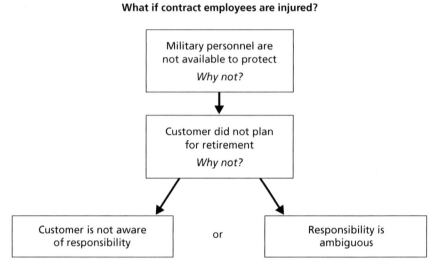

What if contract employees are injured?

> Military personnel are
> not available to protect
> *Why not?*

> Customer did not plan
> for retirement
> *Why not?*

> Customer is not aware   or   Responsibility is
> of responsibility   ambiguous

NOTE: Though not founded on a specific example, this scenario draws from stated
concerns about safety and Army preparedness.
RAND *MG282-3.6*

could leave the military vulnerable or unprepared in other mission-
oriented dimensions. Moreover, an inadequate coordination of force
protection measures and contract activities could cause the apparent
nonperformance of the contractor—e.g., owing to its employees'
inability to get past ID checks or through roadblocks to make deliveries.

Even this example, though initially appearing to relate only to
contract employees, also speaks to a broader set of risks—i.e., those
originating from potential shortcomings in the planning and coordination processes that support the operation. In this case, the example
points to the importance of coordinating roles in-theater, which, in
turn, points to the importance of understanding and adequately
accounting for resource requirements in planning for and establishing
an operation. As above, visibility is an important consideration and
may be somewhat more challenging under contract provisions. However, even with clear visibility, not all dangers are knowable in an

uncertain operating environment. Figure 3.6 depicts a particular causal chain, but not every injury is the result of a failure of policy or practice. Despite carefully considered preparations, an employee may experience a freak accident or become entangled in some other situation too unpredictable to guard against. Given the Army's contractual commitment to providing force protection under the BSC, it might be necessary to establish an ongoing process for reviewing its force protection requirements, with a backup plan for meeting new needs as they arise.

The foregoing examples provide insight into the risk-management methodology as it might apply to a CSS contract, such as the BSC. They suggest the importance of drilling down from proximate to root causes to help identify appropriate mitigation strategies. In each case, stopping at the first layer of causality might lead the analyst to recommend an ineffective or even harmful approach.

As a closely related matter, the examples also illustrate the distinction between contract risks and risks that arise from particular activities or the operating environment more generally. Only some risks are truly contractual. A poorly articulated request can yield seemingly inadequate service in almost any arrangement, be it contractual, MOU, or otherwise. Moreover, the basic incentive to gold plate might exist—and possibly prevail—regardless of the Army's sourcing decision. Even the "injury" example speaks to noncontract risks—i.e., those relating to the planning and coordination processes that should support activities in-theater.

In each case, had the employment of a contractor been incorrectly identified as the underlying or root cause of the potential hazard, the chosen solution might have been to replace the contractor with troops. However, as these simple scenarios show, if the source of the risk resides in the form or content of the request, the customer's operating incentives, or the Army's planning and coordination processes, a simple replacement strategy would not act as an effective risk control. At best, simply replacing contract employees with troops would leave the customer no better off. In fact, it might even leave the customer worse off.

The foregoing examples suggest that a given set of risks may present itself in the operating environment or theater. Choosing a source, with accompanying oversight and management mechanisms, alters the fault trees for theater activities by addressing the underlying hazards in particular ways. Each choice of a source and coordination mechanism gives rise to an associated fault tree. In principle, we can compare fault trees across alternative sources and assess the differences. Alternatively stated, we can imagine any sourcing option in terms of a set of comparisons from a baseline, which could be defined in terms of organic provision or any other set of arrangements, including the status quo. A fault tree analysis relevant to the sourcing decision would focus on comparisons from the baseline.

In summary, this section offers a framework for assessing causality, which also sheds light on the ways in which choices among sourcing options and coordination mechanisms can affect risk. But establishing causality is only part of the risk-management process, regardless of the source. The next step is to assess probability and severity. Indeed, a more comprehensive application of fault tree analysis would have included a probability assessment at each point in the casual chain. It would have indicated the likelihood of each "cause" or event occurring, leading up to the final hazard.[6] Explicit consideration of the likelihood—and the importance—of an event enables resource prioritization. Many things can go wrong, but only some things are server or likely enough to require an *ex ante* response.

Earlier, we described a matrix tool for systematically assessing the probability and severity of potential hazards. The approach can be used to develop a prioritized list of risks. It requires little in the way of direct quantification. Rather, it relies heavily on qualitative assessments formed from expert opinion. However, some of the underlying information required to form an opinion may be hard to find. Examples of such information include the frequency, duration, and cost of

---

[6] Referring to Figure 3.6: what is the probability that the Army is unaware of its force protection responsibility or that the responsibility is ambiguous; what is the probability that the Army will not assign protection; what is the probability that the contractor will be put in harm's way?

various types of failures and the funds, manpower, and other resources required to correct them.

Moreover, most if not all the evidence at our disposal—e.g., in GAO reports, performance evaluation scores, Army observations, and press reports—is outcome-oriented or ex post facto. That is, it already embodies or reflects the Army's efforts to control risk. As such, the evidence says more about the Army's choice of risk controls, its decisions about accepting residual risks, the results of those decisions, and its willingness to live with the consequences than it does about underlying conditions.[7]

Taking this final consideration into account, we defer a more substantive assessment of the evidence on probability and severity to a later discussion of contract outcomes and the Army's treatment of residual risk in the BSC. This discussion follows naturally from a review of the approaches that the Army has taken to managing risks in the contract, including a comparison to the doctrinal ideal. In essence, we look first at how the Army has sought to manage its risks and then we look at the results for lessons learned. Through this examination, we also complete the methodological loop. We draw together the analytical techniques that support the five-step process and apply them to reports of actual incidents, complaints, or concerns.

Risk Management Strategies and Tools in the BSC

Army and joint doctrines call for an explicit and continuous process of risk management, from the earliest phases of planning through the final phases of implementation. A close examination of official BSC documents, as well as CETAC and contractor interviews, suggests that most risk management in the BSC has occurred either intermittently and explicitly (e.g., during the source-selection process) or con-

---

[7] Even if "ex ante" evidence were available, its predictive power might be limited. The limits derive not only from the inherent nature of uncertainty, but also from the difficulty of establishing appropriate analogies. As discussed at the outset of this report, evidence relating to the current contract may provide little insight to the "start up" of an entirely new contract because it was built on several years of prior experience in the Balkans region and elsewhere.

tinuously and implicitly (e.g., within the structure and operation of the contract itself). Risk management may also have occurred through institutional redundancies. Alternative sources of capacity, including other potential contractors and military resources, such as RED HORSE teams, can provide backstops or fail-safe mechanisms if the Army and those responsible for the alternative sources coordinate their planning.[8] In the following two subsections, we address risk assessment and risk mitigation in the BSC.

Risk Assessment. The most visible example of risk assessment occurs in the RFP, which calls for an explicit consideration of performance risk in selecting a contractor. Although sometimes it is treated as a separate evaluation factor in source selections, the Army chose to include performance risk as an element for consideration in evaluating all factors.[9]

Both the language of the RFP and discussions with the Army suggest that the primary concern in the source selection was ensuring that each bidder understood the work scope and that each bidder knew what was expected of it. Consistent with the earlier discussion, in which we noted that there were performance-related hazards, hence risks, associated with each element of the WBS, the Army developed a risk-assessment process that effectively consisted of a point-by-point walk-through of the work scope, asking how well the bidder had addressed each part of it.[10] The risk assessment appears to have been systematic and comprehensive. Nevertheless, some benefit may accrue in drawing more directly from the risk-management methodologies found in Department of the Army (1998b) and

---

[8] "RED HORSE" stands for Rapid Engineer Deployable Heavy Operational Repair Squadron, Engineering. Were the Army to rely on RED HORSE teams as a backstop, it would need to coordinate with the Air Force.

[9] Without a specific mention of "risk," concerns about uncertainty also entered the source-selection process through the consideration of the bidders' management and execution plans. For manpower utilization, CETAC asked each firm to "Discuss your staffing plan to accommodate normal fluctuating workloads in order to maintain an experienced work force during troop surge periods."

[10] Evaluators rated risk as "low," "moderate," or "high" in source selection worksheets. See CETAC (1997).

Department of the Army et al. (2001)—e.g., by tracking the assessment to a list of prioritized WBS elements, ranked by level of risk and concern.

Risk assessment, either explicit or implicit, may have influenced the formulation of the RFP, judging from the structure of the contract and the phrasing of the source-selection criteria. (We discuss the contract's structure, below, in the context of "risk mitigation.") Regarding selection criteria, concerns about quality, including non-performance, permeate each evaluation factor, even the cost factor. For example, the cost factor makes specific reference to the firm's "financial capability" and requires a review of the firm's financial statements, thus implying concern about the potential for nonperformance relating to insolvency. The early history of contract activity in the Balkans suggests the origins of this concern. KBR, the first LOGCAP contractor, is reported to have been financing its own operations—without timely payments from the government—at the outset of the Balkans operation in FY 1996.

The source-selection criteria provide less indication of concern about cost as it relates to actual spending levels, perhaps reflecting an assessment that quality was of greater concern. Nonperformance or inadequate performance may have been deemed more significant hazards than cost overruns. The RFP offers the following guidance: "In making the comparison [of bids,] the Government is more concerned with obtaining superior technical or management features than with making an award at the lowest overall cost to the Government. However, the Government will not make an award at a significantly higher overall cost to the Government to achieve slightly superior technical or management features." It also states that, *All evaluation factors other than cost or price, when combined, are significantly more important than cost or price"* (emphasis in original).

Interestingly, the cost factor does not address the level of costs directly. Rather, it refers to the "overall reasonableness" of the firms' proposals, including concerns about realism, completeness, and financial capability. Not surprisingly, the "management and execution plan" factor focuses on process: "describe your overall plan for accomplishing this project in the most cost-effective and efficient manner" and "describe your approach to estimating and controlling project costs and how you would propose updating the estimates to reflect cost data and changes."

In contrast to the doctrinal call for risk management in the earliest phases of planning, we have little evidence of formal risk assessment in the initial decision to reobtain contract support in the Balkans in 1998—i.e., the "make-or-buy" decision. GAO's explanation of the justification for the sole-source contract strongly suggests the Army considered the risks of shifting from KBR to a different contractor, preferring to stick with a known quantity, but it does not provide insight into whether the Army evaluated risks in the underlying make-or-buy decision, including the subsidiary decisions to include or exclude certain activities from the WBS. Similarly, the RFP's explicit call for experience "especially in the Balkans region" may reflect a preference for a particular contractor or type of contractor but does not speak to the relative risks of choosing between contract and organic support. However, the concept of "initial" is muddy in this case because the BSC emerged from two previous contracts. A proper evaluation of the role of risk assessment in planning, particularly the fundamental make-or-buy decision, would require careful consideration of the initial decision to rely on the LOGCAP contract in 1995 and the issuance of the sole-source contract in 1997.

Although not formally framed as a risk assessment, ongoing decisions about sourcing new work offer evidence of efforts to assess risk. These decisions occur through the JARB validation and source-selection processes. Although the JARB implementing instructions do not explicitly address risk, the concept runs implicitly through the text. The instructions provide examples of suggested questions that board members should ask during the JARB process to evaluate the necessity of the proposed requirement, the availability of funds, the cost and quality of service, and the context of the requirement. Some questions relevant to the cost and quality of service include the following:

- What is the funding source for the requirement?
- Was this item in your budget?

- How have you gotten along without it for so long?
- Why is this a valid requirement?
- Why won't a cheaper version suit the need? (Remember that cheaper sometimes means more expensive in the long run, if lower-quality products must be replaced more quickly.)
- Is the vendor or contractor you recommend the best source/only source you looked at?
- Is this part of a larger project? Will any other purchases need to be made to produce a complete and useable facility or to produce a complete and functional system?

Some but not all of the questions can be reframed in terms of risk assessment. For example, the inquiry into the suitability of cheaper versions addresses quality and cost risk through the possibility of trade-offs between cost and quality. The first two questions address the availability of funding, essentially asking, "Will you be able to pay for this?" or "Are you facing or will you create a resource risk?" The last question addresses integration. Though stated in terms of a product acquisition, it applies equally to services, "Is there a risk of inadequate integration with other services?"

Risk Mitigation. The primary risk-mitigation tools appear to be imbedded in the structure and operating principles of the contract. The BSC attempts to balance concerns about preparedness and flexibility through its preplanned performance-based work scope, IDIQ specification, and CPAF payment structure. This formulation provides some of the assurances of advance planning while accommodating operational uncertainty and allowing the contractor to draw on the full extent of its corporate resources, including its expertise. On the one hand, the contractor stands ready to respond to a wide range of possible customer needs, having previously mapped out its approach or identified certain key assets, including personnel. On the other hand, it is not locked into a particular course of action.

The contract's built-in management and oversight mechanisms, including CDRL reports and work order, funding, and award fee processes, also serve as potential risk-mitigation tools. CDRL reports provide a nearly continuous flow of information for monitoring the contractor's performance, potentially serving as an early warning system for CETAC and other contract participants. Not everyone on each CDRL report distribution list necessarily reads every report that is sent, but Army comments indicate that key reports are scanned regularly for significant anomalies. The work order, funding, and award fee processes provide opportunities for timely evaluations of performance and identification of shortcomings. Moreover, in the context of orders for new work, the JARB's source-selection process may mitigate some cost- and quality-related performance risks by posing the option of alternative suppliers. To the extent that the threat of the Army's choosing an alternative supplier—be it organic, host nation, or contract—is credible, the selection process may induce competition among suppliers and improve their performance.

The ASGs, JARB, and AFEB serve risk-mitigating functions through their coordinating roles. Each of these institutions brings participants together to address different aspects of the contractual relationship. To the extent that the ASGs have taken on some of the broader roles of the BCCA, which existed explicitly for the purposes of coordinating base camp activities, they may play a vital role. The BCCA previously approved some work orders, but it also played a larger part in base camp coordination overall. Unlike the AFEB and JARB, it may have provided a significant opportunity for a two-way flow of information and ideas between U.S. government personnel and the contractor and its employees. It may have promoted cohesion. By comparison, the JARB and AFEB have more narrowly focused roles in the acquisition and evaluation processes, respectively. Nevertheless, merely bringing many participants together in one place at one time, even if they are primarily U.S. government participants, can facilitate broader coordination.

Outside of these formal channels, placing a priority on day-to-day communication can also mitigate risk. Working together cohesively, Army personnel and contractor employees may be better able to solve problems and identify opportunities as they arise. As noted previously, Army doctrine describes the benefits of developing "habitual relationships" to foster cooperation and build trust. Although this concept most typically relates to system support, the long-standing nature of the BSC may offer a reasonable analogy. Over time, both the customer and KBR have sought to improve channels of communication, both formally and informally. Conversations with both parties suggest that they have had success in this arena in that seemingly open communication channels have contributed to solving problems and identifying opportunities.

Perhaps the most consequential elements of the Army's risk-mitigation strategy emerged before the contract took effect, in the design of the source-selection process. As already noted, the source selection called for financial capability to mitigate the risk of liquidity- or bankruptcy-based nonperformance. Experience and past performance were weighted heavily in the competition, leading to the decision to continue with the incumbent contractor. Though potentially fostering cooperation and building trust, an incumbency-based approach presents risks of its own. In particular, if the threat of choosing an alternative source induces competition and improves performance, then the absence of that threat might have the opposite effect. Any incumbent—be it organic, host nation, or contractor—may become complacent if it perceives the absence of real competition. The customer may greatly reduce the probability of a severely negative outcome, but it also may obtain acceptable rather than outstanding service, possibly at a higher cost than necessary, absent other incentives. Thus, reliance on long-term relationships may place an additional burden on award fee evaluation processes and other day-to-day management and oversight tools.

Finally, another risk-mitigation tool involves the use of internal and external evaluations and audits. In the vocabulary of the five-step risk-management process in Department of the Army (1998b) and Department of the Army et al. (2001), shown in Figure 3.1, these types of activities would fall under step five, "Supervise and Review," which links back to step three, "Develop Controls and Make Risk Decisions." Responding to feedback and developing new controls are crucial elements of the five-step process. GAO's examination of the initial Balkans contracts and the BSC in particular provided insight and offered recommendations that reportedly motivated the Army to modify some of its management and oversight practices, including its award fee criteria and scoring methods. GAO, therefore, might be considered part of the risk-mitigation process. We address the reports' findings and consequences in more detail below in the context of the BSC track record.

Assessing the BSC Track Record

To complete the methodological loop, we examine the BSC track record in light of the doctrinal five-step process and the Army's own selection of risk-management tools and look for opportunities to enhance the performance of CSS contracts. Caveats on data availability and ex-post evidence notwithstanding, we look to GAO reports about the BSC, performance evaluation scores, interviews with Army officials and contractors, and press reports for insight into the causality, probability, and severity of a variety of hazards and, perhaps more directly, the results of the Army's application of the foregoing risk controls and its tolerance of residual risk. We draw together the analytical techniques that we introduced in the preceding sections, by applying them to reports of actual incidents, complaints, or concerns.

In general, we find that most of the concerns voiced about this contract relate to performance, security, or a combination of both, and only some are presented with supporting evidence. Under the broad rubric of performance, we find references to activity-level concerns about quality, including fundamental reliability, and to cost. Three commonly cited GAO reports address performance in terms of costs, quality of life, and readiness. Higher-order concerns about security have tended to relate to the safety of contract employees and the attendant need for force protection. More recently, attention has also turned to the troops' safety and how contract employees, particularly foreign nationals, might affect it. However, "references to concerns" and empirical evidence are not the same thing; authors, interviewees, and other commentators may voice their concerns, but only some provide evidence of probability or severity.

Concerns About Performance

Three GAO reports speak to concerns about BSC performance. One report addresses costs, "Army Should Do More to Control Contract Costs in the Balkans" (GAO, 2000a). A second report addresses quality, "Quality of Life for U.S. Soldiers Deployed in the Balkans" (GAO, 2000b). A third report, "Contractors Provide Vital Services to Deployed Forces but Are Not Adequately Addressed in [DoD] Plans" (GAO, 2003), looks at contracting risks across services and venues, especially as they relate to readiness. First, we turn to the report on cost (GAO, 2000a) and evaluate its findings and consequences in view of the five-step risk-management process and the Army's approach to risk assessment and mitigation. Next, we examine the report on quality of life (GAO, 2000b), also in terms of doctrine and practice. We use the third report (GAO, 2003) as a point of departure for a discussion of readiness, focusing on the contractor's ability or willingness to provide services.

GAO's report on controlling contract costs addresses two types of concerns about costs: those relating to specific incidents of possible overspending and those relating to contract management, oversight, and cost controls more generally.[11] Turning to the first type, GAO addresses four specific instances of possible cost excesses involving the following: firefighting services, power generation, base camp personalization, and furniture orders. Using the vocabulary of the risk-management framework, the reported cost excesses would be described as activity-level hazards. Here, we evaluate the reported cost excesses through the lens of that framework. Drawing from the main text of the GAO report, we list each reported cost excess, assess its cause or causes, and evaluate its severity in terms of cost in Table 3.1.

Table 3.1, row one, partially fulfills the requirements of step one of the five-step process, "Identify Hazards." However, in this retrospective, or *ex post,* setting, row one lists *actual* reported negative out-

---

[11] GAO's cost control analysis features prominently in many press reports. It appears to have provided the basis for many public claims of excess spending. We have seen little or no independent analysis from other external—i.e., noncontract and nonmilitary—sources.

Table 3.1
Assessment of GAO Cost Study

	Firefighting Service	Power Generation	Personalization	Furniture
Reported cost excess	Planned firefighting services too costly; potentially unsupportable	Power generation too costly	Unnecessary spending on changes to personalize base camps	Unnecessary spending on furniture (ordered outside of BSC; processed and assembled under BSC)
Proximate cause(s)	Contractor proposed too many firefighters and fire engines, ultimately reduced but did not eliminate "gap"; base not large enough to support proposed staffing and equipment	Contractor provided "excess" redundancy; leasing decisions	Contractor made changes to personalize camps at unit rotations—e.g., new signs with new unit insignia, renaming streets, rearranging office space	Customer purchased furniture that was unusable, owing to lack of space in Southeast Asia huts (SEA-huts)
Intermediate cause(s)	Disagreement over staffing and equipment requirements; differences in Army and civilian training requirements; differences in Army and commercial or municipal service standards, so that contractor planned for higher level	Difference between "best business practices" and Army requirements; differences in perceived benefits of leasing	Customer issued large number of work orders and service requests for changes	
Root cause(s)	Inadequate communication between customer and service provider; lack of agreed service standards, possibly coupled with contractor and customer incentives to "gold plate"; difference in local and military wage rates	Inadequate communication between customer and service provider; lack of agreed redundancy standards, possibly coupled with contractor and customer incentives to "gold plate"	Contractor and customer incentives to "gold plate"	Customer did not review match of purchases to requirements

Table 3.1—continued

	Firefighting Service	Power Generation	Personalization	Furniture
Fault summary	Planning and coordination; quality and cost trade-offs; incentives	Planning and coordination; quality and cost trade-offs; incentives	Quality and cost trade-offs; incentives	Planning and coordination; poorly framed request
Severity	In dollar terms, the staffing debate appears to have come down to 11 "excess" firefighters; amounting to about $150,000 per year, valued at local wages[a]; insufficient data to estimate costs of equipment or support consideration[b]	GAO reports that terminating 38 "excess" leases would result in annual savings of $5.1 million and purchasing 48 previously leased generators would save another $85 million over five years	No cost data available	Unspecified share of $5.2 million spent outside of BSC on furniture for SEA-huts; $377,000 on BSC for processing and assembling

SOURCE: Authors' analysis of GAO (2000a, pp. 11–16).
[a] CETAC reports local labor costs ranging from $1.25 per hour for basic laborers to $5.00 per hour for construction supervisors; we apply a wage rate of $1.50 per hour and assume coverage 24 hours a day, seven days a week.
[b] Had the initial plan been accepted, absent debate or modification, the "excess" would have amounted to 50 firefighters, with associated costs in excess of $650,000 per year.

comes. These outcomes are the by-products of prior Army decisions to manage risks in a particular way.

Rows two to five fulfill another requirement of step one, by listing the causes of each negative outcome. Taken in order, from rows two to four, down each column, they resemble a fault tree by drilling down from proximate to root causes. As posited in the earlier exploration of illustrative scenarios, a cursory look at proximate causes alone could result in inappropriate management responses. In all but one case, the proximate cause is an action taken by the contractor. However, in all cases, the root cause derives from either a planning and coordination or incentives problem, typically involving both the contractor and the customer. The causal chains associated with the firefighting services and power generation examples speak to the gaps left by inadequate planning, coordination, and communication and the role that incentives can play in filling them. In the case of power generation, absent an agreed-on redundancy standard, the contractor chose to minimize the risk of power outages and apply "best business practices" by providing 100 percent, across-the-board backup. Given the contract's CPAF structure and the quality-focused nature of the performance review process, which then sought to avoid negative surprises, the result was unsurprising.

The result is equally unsurprising in the case of the planned "overprovision" of firefighting services. However, in this case, the stipulation of a performance standard might not have affected the contractor's proposed approach. Given the relatively low cost of labor in the local population and its relative lack of skills, it might be more cost-effective for the contractor to hire more firefighters, drawing from that population, than the Army would hire, were it drawing from its own ranks. To the extent that the contractor and the Army are drawing from different labor pools with different wage and skill profiles, there is no reason to expect them to make the same staffing decisions. Given these differences, responding directly to the proximate cause—e.g., by imposing Army planning factors on the contractor—could result in inappropriate hiring decisions, yield a higher risk of fire damage, and potentially raise costs.

The third and fourth examples are analytically simpler. In the case of the base camp changes, the Army asked for the personalization service, presumably to satisfy the end user, and paid for it—that is, it got what it asked for but may have asked for too much. Regarding the furniture, again the Army got what it asked for, but, in this case, it asked for the wrong thing. The Army failed to review its furniture purchase orders in light of its requirements, which led to a mismatch.

Table 3.1, row six, evaluates severity, which is the first requirement of step two, "Assess Hazards." With the exception of "power generation too costly," the cost implications of the negative outcomes listed in row one appear to be modest, especially in relation to total contract spending, which amounted to about $455 million in FY 2000. Even including the power generation example, the reported excesses appear to have been amenable to timely correction.

Though they are not depicted in Table 3.1, the GAO report also raises more general concerns about management and oversight, especially as they pertain to recurring costs.[12] The report argued that the Army should "place greater emphasis on the level and efficiency with which recurring services are provided," making the point that once new recurring services are established, delivery tends to proceed on something close to autopilot. Drawing on those concerns, the report appears to support the adoption of standards for both the amount and cost-effectiveness of service provision, which together could specify both "what" and "how." To adopt standards for the former could serve to support a performance-based contract, depending on the need for specificity, but to adopt standards for the latter could undermine its operation and potentially yield new risks. In particular, a potential benefit of the performance-based contract is to enable the contractor to adapt and respond to changing circumstances.

Given the level of generality of the concerns about management and oversight—GAO provides some detail for just one example, involving alleged overstaffing—it is difficult to reframe them in terms of the five-step process. Broadly stated, the hazard might be "excess

---

[12] See GAO (2000a, pp. 16–18) for a fuller discussion.

recurring costs"; the proximate cause might be "unnecessary or inefficient provision of recurring services"; the intermediate cause might be "absence of standards" or "insufficient oversight"; and the root causes might be "customer's intent to reduce its role in CSS provision and refrain from micromanagement," coupled with various quality- and CPAF-related incentives. For example, a higher negotiated cost estimate, tied to a higher-quality service, could yield a higher award fee payment. Per step two of the five-step process, GAO does not explicitly assess "severity" of this hazard but offers evidence that recurring costs constitute the lion's share of total spending on the contract and might therefore shelter considerable excesses.

Neither Table 3.1 nor our assessment of GAO's concerns about recurring costs says much about ex-ante risk—i.e., the underlying or inherent risk of excess expenditures. However, both analyses provide insight into the Army's choice of risk controls, specifically its tolerance for and acceptance of residual risk, and the implementation of those controls. Choice and implementation are the cornerstones of step three, "Develop Controls and Make Risk Decisions," and step four, "Implement Controls." With hindsight, the observed cost phenomena appear to reflect or be consistent with the Army's implied tolerance of residual risk, including a willingness to accept a nonzero probability of excess cost, and a preference for quality when faced with a potential trade-off.

The mere existence of the GAO report speaks to step five of the five-step process, "Supervise and Review," including "New Controls." Through its evaluation and reporting processes, GAO provided feedback to the Army, which apparently resulted in the design and implementation of new controls. GAO provided this step because it found that, at least for the activities detailed in its report, the Army had not.

Apparently in response to GAO's concerns, the Army returned to step three, "Develop Controls and Make Risk Decision," and took several steps to reduce costs. Among them, it substantially modified its performance review process. As addressed previously, cost, especially cost *reduction*, gained new prominence, both quantitatively and qualitatively. Recall that "funds management and cost control" account for 40 percent of the contractor's overall evaluation score, up from 30 percent. Qualitatively, the emphasis of the process shifted from staying within projections—a top score previously required few if any negative surprises—to reducing costs. Top scores also require continuous improvements. To earn an overall point score of 95 percent or better—constituting an "outstanding" rating—the contractor must show new additional cost savings in each review period.[13]

Shortly predating the publication of the GAO report, USAREUR issued a call to "conduct quarterly reviews of ongoing recurring service being performed by the contractor to ensure that only essential services are being demanded," which it later sought to strengthen (GAO 2000a, p. 20). The Army also reconciled contractor WBS with "Blue Book" and "Red Book" standards for CSS and facilities, respectively.[14] Though not dictating "how" to provide services or build facilities, the volumes do address "what." The Blue Book, more formally known as "The USAREUR Blue Book: Base Camp Baseline Standards—A Guide to Base Operations Downrange," is a relatively recent innovation. Its development, in conjunction with the newly initiated ongoing service reviews, may have been directly responsive to GAO's concerns about service levels and some of the specific "excesses." However, the Army appears to have chosen to address concerns about efficiency primarily through its newly reformulated evaluation process. The call for ongoing cost reductions would tend to drive out waste. GAO (2000a, p. 20) also reports that the Army intended to "mandate that officials in Kosovo and Macedonia identify $40 million in cost savings for fiscal year 2001."

Figure 3.7 shows the contractor's ratings over time. The scoring changes—new brackets, weights, and cost criteria—were first announced in February 2002 and applied at the award fee evaluation board meeting held in June 2002. Having already declined from early

---

[13] "Outstanding" is now the highest ratings bracket. Previously, the top bracket was "above average."

[14] USAREUR must approve any exceptions to those standards.

Figure 3.7
Evaluation Scores

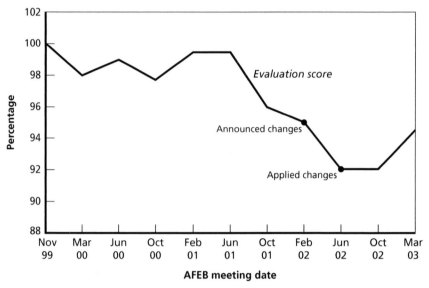

SOURCE: CETAC financial records, provided May 2003.
RAND MG282-3.7

2001 to early 2002, KBR's score dropped further in June 2002, albeit remaining in the "excellent" range, with evidence of a rebound in March 2003. It is difficult to attribute the June 2002 decline to any one factor, given the simultaneous introduction of three potentially significant changes.

Concerns about cost notwithstanding, the Army appears to be generally satisfied with the service it receives from the BSC contractor; first, as evidenced by the contractor's performance ratings, which, as shown in Figure 3.7, have not once dropped below the numeric equivalent of "excellent" even at their nadir, and second, as evidenced by the findings of the GAO report (2000b), "Quality of Life for U.S. Soldiers Deployed in the Balkans." In assessing the quality of life in the Balkans, the report surveys the BSC's ultimate "end users"—i.e., the troops in the field—and addresses a variety of services. Some, such as food and laundry services, are covered under the BSC. The report concludes, "The vast majority of soldiers we surveyed said the

Army's efforts met or exceeded their quality of life expectations."
Regarding food service specifically, "More than 90 percent of the soldiers rated food service at their camp as excellent, very good, or satisfactory. . . . Unit officials in Bosnia said that the quantity and quality
of the food is so good that personnel are gaining weight."

GAO's findings on quality of life in the Balkans provide further
ex-post evidence of the Army's tolerance for and acceptance of residual risk. Consistent with our assessment of the Army's approach to
risk management—i.e., its concern for quality in the formulation,
award, and implementation of the BSC, GAO found a high level of
customer satisfaction with respect to quality. Given the underlying
premise of an inherent trade-off between quality and cost and the
Army's unstated objective of reducing its role in CSS provision, we
would expect to see a relatively low tolerance for quality-related risks,
with very little slippage, and a relatively high tolerance for cost-related
risks that might allow acceptance of some "excess" cost.

The Army's response to GAO's reports and any subsequent cost
savings may suggest the merit of GAO's concerns, but an assessment
of cost savings, absent the context of the contract's other goals, may
effectively overvalue those savings by failing to account for potential
noncost trade-offs. For example, to obtain savings, the Army might
need to apply additional resources, primarily manpower and leadership focus, to contract management, or reduce quality. Given competing demands on these resources, the Army might choose to pay a
premium—in the form of forgone savings—to implement a contract
that reduces demands and maintains quality. More generally, the
Army, or any other customer, might choose to trade some cost risk to
meet other objectives. Indeed, the BSC's record, as exhibited in
GAO's report on costs, KBR's ratings history, and GAO's quality-of-
life survey, bears this out. In some instances, it might be preferable to
choose to respond and recover rather than impose ex-ante controls,
particularly controls that might engender new risks.

However, the question remains about the appropriate balance
between cost and other objectives, such as reducing demands on
Army manpower. Restated in terms of the risk-management framework, the Army must decide how much cost-related risk to accept as

"residual" and how much to mitigate, given that mitigation of one risk may place additional demands on already scarce resources or exacerbate another risk. Whether the Army initially accepted too much of any one type of residual risk would depend on whether the incremental benefits of mitigation would have outweighed the incremental cost, after accounting for other contract rationale.

Finally, in commenting on the chain of events, the depiction of the Army's reprioritization of cost as solely responsive to GAO's concerns might give short shrift to the temporal or evolutionary dimension of risk management. The Army may have been responding to congressional pressure, but it may also have been undertaking its own version of step three, "Supervise and Review," in response to changing needs. One could well imagine a customer placing the highest priority on getting the job done and supporting the mission at the start of an operation and then choosing to return later, after conditions had stabilized, to hone its management practices.

The third GAO report (2003), "Contractors Provide Vital Services to Deployed Forces but Are Not Adequately Addressed in DOD Plans," though addressing a larger group of contracts, raises an additional and arguably more fundamental concern about performance, that of the contractor's readiness to provide services. Can or will the contractor respond when needed or called on? In this regard, the question is not just, "Will the road be bumpy?" It is, "Will the road be built?" Or "Will the contractor show up?" If the contractor does not show up, "Does the customer have a 'Plan B'?"

GAO (2003, pp. 12–13) notes that DOD Instruction 3020.37 assigns responsibilities and prescribes procedures to implement DoD policy to ensure that components develop and implement plans and procedures intended to provide reasonable assurance of the continuation of essential services during crisis situations and prepare a contingency plan for obtaining the essential service from alternative sources when reasonable doubt crops up about the continuation of that service. Accordingly, the component is responsible for identifying services that are mission essential and designating them in the contract statement of work. When a reasonable assurance of continuation of essential contract services cannot be attained, the component activity commander is to do one of three things:

- Make the transition to an alternative source.
- Prepare a contingency plan.
- Accept the risk.

Readiness, in this context, relates to a host of other factors, including the preparedness of the contractor, the flexibility of the contract vehicle, the authority of the TF commander and other chain-of-command issues, the extent of cohesion across military and contract personnel, funding, and the willingness of the contractor to provide services in a hostile environment.

Indeed, in conducting this analysis, we have found it difficult to separate the discussion of the contractor's readiness from the discussion of the safety of its employees because both issues are elements of a dynamic system that, under some circumstances, may also involve the overall readiness of the force. For example, the contractor's willingness to provide service in a hostile environment may depend, in part, on whether it perceives that it is adequately protected, but the requirement for providing that protection may divert troops from other core functions. As we have noted previously and will address again below, the net resource or manpower effect of CSS contracting may be favorable nevertheless, but an unanticipated force protection requirement may be problematic, especially in the short run.

What does the evidence say about readiness in the BSC? For the most part, the BSC appears to be a reliable and responsive arrangement; there have been few reports of lack of preparedness or inflexibility. Indeed, both the Army and the contractor report rapid turnaround times on NTPs, implementation, and definitization of work orders. On a potentially larger scale, we see evidence of agility in the geographically changing nature of the contract. Initially, in early 1999, the BSC called for service provision in the Houston home office, Hungary, Bosnia, and Croatia. Soon thereafter, given significant operational changes, the list grew to include other countries in the region, including Albania, Greece, and Macedonia.

However, reaching even further back into KBR's Balkans tenure reveals a possible exception—the LOGCAP start-up in late 1995. During the initial phases of the operation, the Air Force's RED HORSE teams and the Navy's Seabees were called on to provide added support. Whether this was a preplanned measure or a stopgap remains unclear.[15] If the RED HORSE teams' and Seabees' contributions were a stopgap, then events provide evidence that the Army was either very lucky that the Air Force and Navy resources were available when called on or it had a viable "Plan B." Also in the early days of LOGCAP's engagement in the Balkans, we heard a report of a funding lag. In particular, one interviewee noted that KBR initially self-financed its operations while awaiting U.S. government payments.

Turning to more recent events, the evidence relating to operations in Afghanistan and Iraq requires further consideration. For example, the same press report that begins, "U.S. troops in Iraq suffered through months of unnecessarily poor living conditions because some civilian contractors hired by the Army for logistics support failed to show up," citing a top-ranking Army official, also includes a statement from an Army contracting official that "he knew of no hesitation or lateness by KBR civilian contractors" (D. Wood, 2003; *BusinessWeek*, 2003). That press report also cites the difficulties in obtaining affordable insurance for contract employees in high-risk environments as a possible delaying factor. While Army doctrine provides guidance on this issue, we do not know whether measures were taken to implement the guidance.[16]

On balance, the available evidence suggests that the BSC has been a "ready" arrangement in the context of an ongoing operations but that start-ups may pose significant challenges, not because of the use of contracts per se, but because of more onerous planning, coor-

---

[15] See http://www.globalsecurity.org/military/facility/bosnia.htm for a description of "construction delays and base services management growing pains," which suggests it was a stopgap.

[16] With regard to "Personal Readiness," Department of the Army (2003, p. 3-7) notes, "Contractor employees also need to be advised that personal life insurance coverage may be limited or denied in certain military-related operations. When this is the case, the government is prepared to underwrite the insurance to enable coverage to continue."

dination, and management requirements, some relating to funding and security. This does not imply that contracts and contractors cannot be put to good—i.e., reliable—use in the early phases of an operation, but that the customer must be in a position to plan for, coordinate, and manage them. Indeed, such concerns can be generalized to noncontract environments. The relative costs of alternatives are important as well. Even if arrangements ensure that a contractor can react with a short response time, it might be cheaper to leave very short turn-time events to active military forces, which are standing ready at all times. However, if the function is in the reserve components, then timing and cost may also be as issue.

To what extent are concerns about nonperformance strictly about the use of contractors, or more generally about readiness of the force? Loosely applying the fault tree concept, Table 3.2 compares and contrasts some possible causes for contract and organic source nonperformance. Performance failures, including unavailability and inability to perform services, may arise from planning or implementation failures.

One point raised above in the text and in Table 3.2 is "customer ability." The customer must be able to plan for, coordinate, and manage the contract. As noted before, adequate training and institutional memory are important but may be lacking. Various GAO

Table 3.2
Comparison of Potential Sources of Nonperformance Relating to Planning and Implementation

Contractor	Organic
TAA, PPBES, operational plans/ operational orders do not support	TAA, PPBES, operational plans/ operational orders do not support
Contract misstates requirements or provides inadequate incentives	Operational plans/operational orders misstate requirements
Faulty source selection—e.g., omits key criteria	Poor match of resources to requirements
Processes are inflexible	Processes are inflexible
Customer misuses contract vehicle—training is necessary	Troops do not know how to provide services—training is necessary

NOTE: Nonperformance could include failure to arrive on time or inability to perform a task. TAA = Total Army Authorized; PPBES = Planning, Programming, Budgeting, and Execution System.

reports have addressed these and similar concerns. Although the BSC appears not to have suffered dramatically from planning, coordination, or management failures, it had several years to evolve and mature. Other contracts in other venues may not have this advantage.

To conclude, one arena in which the risks associated with contracting appear to be profoundly different from those associated with organic provision is in the chain of command, both with respect to the contractor and its employees. As reported in Department of the Army (2003, p. 4-12), the contractor's employees do not fall under the military chain of command. In fact, if they did, it could jeopardize their status as civilians accompanying the force. Rather, "maintaining the discipline of contractor employees is the responsibility of the contractor's management structure."[17] And the contractor's management structure is responsible to the contracting authority—e.g., the PCO—and various courts of law. (For more on chain-of-command considerations, see Department of the Army, 1999, p. 14.) Speaking to compliance, Department of the Army (2003, p. 4-11) makes the following observation:

> One of the key elements in the managing of contractors is contract compliance. Contract compliance is simply ensuring that the contractor is doing what the contract requires. The key to effective contract compliance is making sure that planners consider the variety of requirements relating to contract support, include them in operational plans, and communicate these plans to the contracting structure so that they can be included in applicable contracts.

The bottom line: if "it" is not in the contract, then "it" is not enforceable, and, even if it is "enforceable," it is not enforceable through the military chain of command, but through the contracting authority and, if need be, the court system. One important consequence of this is the Army's inability to control the behavior of contract employees when they are on their own time. Reports of alleged

---

[17] "When criminal activity is involved, international agreements and the host-nation's laws take precedence" (Department of the Army, 2003, p. 4-12).

employee misconduct in DynCorp's tenure as the second LOGCAP contractor may speak, in part, to this issue.

Taking a less legalistic view, conversations with both parties to the BSC strongly suggest that another force comes into play in this arena: that of professional reputation and good business practices. To the extent that a contractor wishes to remain in business, maintain or renew an existing contract, or obtain new contracts in the future, employee oversight and compliance should be in its best interest.

Concerns About Safety of Personnel

Dating back to the initial LOGCAP contract, we find references to concerns about security, specifically about the safety of contract employees and the attendant need for force protection. Adding to these concerns, the role of international law may be ambiguous in contingency operations, "The full protections granted to 'prisoners of war' under the Geneva Convention Relative to the Treatment of Prisoners of War . . . and the Hague Convention . . . apply only during an international armed conflict between signatories to those conventions. Accordingly, these conventions are generally inapplicable to military operations other than war." (See Department of the Army, 1998a, p. 5.) Moreover, the status of contract employees as civilians accompanying the force may be ambiguous in other settings, depending on the specific circumstances under which they are employed and local perceptions about the nature of their activities. More recently, in the wake of terrorist attacks overseas and on U.S. soil, Army officials and others have also tended to raise concerns about the safety of U.S. troops vis-á-vis contract employees, especially foreign nationals.

Regarding contract employee safety, we have seen little ex-post evidence of hazards within the operations of the BSC, although we have seen some evidence of a possible increase in risk in the broader context of the regional operating environment in the form of the ambush of a U.N. police officer.[18] With regard to the BSC specifi-

---

[18] An August 2003 report of a U.N. officer killed in an ambush in Kosovo describes the incident as "the first killing of a U.N. police officer on duty in Kosovo since the United

cally, one observer notes incidents of literal highway robbery directed against contract employees but reports no injuries. Nevertheless, the seriousness of the incidents prompted the Army to provide additional protection. At least initially, the response may have diverted troops from other functions.

The unanticipated need for additional protection recalls the discussion of planning and coordination outlined in Figure 3.6. In that figure, we set out a hypothetical scenario involving the injury of a contract employee. We asked why the injury had occurred; ultimately, the answer may have been a planning and coordination failure. As noted in that discussion, the Army cannot foresee all possible dangers, but it must, at the very least, be aware of its protective responsibilities. Such awareness might not have been universal at the outset of the BSC but reportedly has grown. Adequate protection also requires visibility. As a practical matter, the Army may have difficulty protecting the contractor's employees if it lacks knowledge of their whereabouts. In the case of the BSC, the contractor provides regular staffing reports, per the CDRL. Moreover, interviewees have noted that the contractor and its employees maintain close day-to-day communications with their Army counterparts.

As in the hypothetical scenario, it is important to frame the resource aspect of this problem in terms of planning and coordination. Although contract employees may appear to be a resource drain in the moment that troops are diverted to protect them, they may not be. On balance, fewer Army resources—in terms of manpower—may be devoted to protecting contract employees than would be needed to provide the contracted services in their stead. Moreover, were the Army providing its own CSS, some force protection would still be required.

Looking outside the BSC, more recent events in other parts of the world indicate the prevalence of significant threats to safety in some, far less stable operating environments. On August 5, 2003, a

---

Nations assumed control of the Serbian province in 1999." The report draws a connection to a similar but noninjurious attack in May 2003 and refers to a possible increase in anti-U.N. sentiment among Kosovo's ethnic Albanian majority (N. Wood, 2003, p. 9).

U.S. civilian KBR employee was reportedly killed "when the mail truck he was driving was blown up by a homemade explosive north of the town of Tikrit," in a part of Iraq then considered to be part of the war zone (Filkins, 2003). On January 21, 2003, a contractor was killed and another seriously injured in an ambush in Kuwait. According to a press report, they were in Kuwait to work on software installation for the U.S. military (Merle, 2003). According to the same report, "a Dyncorp pilot was killed in January 2002, when the Colombian military destroyed a U.S. government helicopter to keep it from falling into the hands of leftist guerillas." In the more distant past, the report also cites the deaths of three DynCorp employees in a helicopter crash in Peru. Absent more detailed information about these incidents, we cannot apply the five-step process. However, those with access to such information could walk through the analytical process delineated in the hypothetical scenario and above to conduct the assessment independently.

Returning to the issue of readiness, the extent to which safety considerations might affect the willingness of a contract provider and its employees "to show up" would likely depend on their perceptions of the risk level, considering the protective measures, coupled with their tolerance for risk and the compensation that the Army is offering for taking on the risk.[19] If the contractor and its employees believe that the Army is taking adequate steps to ensure an acceptable level of safety or, conversely, residual risk—or is allowing them to take steps of their own—and is providing adequate compensation, given the risk, they may be more willing to show up than otherwise.[20] Such considerations are potentially negotiable and can be articulated in the terms of the contract, at least in theory. However, a time may come when the customer and contractor cannot negotiate such terms satisfactorily—the risks may be too high to support mutually accept-

---

[19] See discussion in Department of the Army (2003, p. 4-10).

[20] The ability of the contractor and its employees to take steps of their own may be constrained by the terms of international law, insofar as the contractor's employees may jeopardize their legal protections by carrying firearms or appearing to behave more like soldiers than like civilians.

able contractual language. The contractor may require more protection or compensation than the customer can feasibly or cost-effectively provide. Clearly, there may be some operating environments in which contractually provided CSS is inappropriate.

Following the attack on the USS *Cole* off Yemen in October 2000 and the September 11, 2001, attacks on the World Trade Center and the Pentagon, the employment of foreign nationals, either through contractors or host nation support, has given rise to additional concerns about the safety of U.S. troops.[21] References to concerns about the potential for terrorist activities—e.g., tampering with food and water supplies—are not unusual. To date, we have little evidence regarding contractor-based terrorist activities directed against U.S. troops.[22] However, we do not have expertise in the evaluation of terrorist threats and leave the probability assessment to those who do. Department of the Army (2003, p. 2-9) refers to the "very real possibility of direct or indirect actions taken against U.S. forces by contractor employees or individuals posing as contractor employees" and offers the following guidance (pp. 6-7 to 6-8):

> Due to recent terrorist activity against U.S. forces, all units must ensure force-protection/antiterrorism plans and actions are integrated into movement and support operations in all areas. Use of local or TCN [third-country national] contractor employees must be carefully considered from the antiterrorism perspective.
>
> Commanders at all levels must include the following areas in force-protection/antiterrorism predeployment planning:
>
> • Threat and vulnerability assessments. Units assess the threat and their own vulnerability prior to deployment. Assessment must include risk of using local national and TCN contractor employees vice using military or U.S. national civilian capabilities.

---

[21] As a practical matter, employing foreign nationals also raises concerns about readiness because "lockdowns" could result in shortages of employees at U.S. facilities.

[22] For example, see Risen and Van Natta (2003, p. 1).

- Security planning. Units must take the results of threat and vulnerability assessment and develop security plans when using local and TCN contractors. Tailored intelligence and counterintelligence support, host-nation assistance, and detailed contractor-employee screening plans must be in place. Special emphasis must be placed on local national and TCN contractor-employee access to vulnerable facilities and areas.
- Combat and Combat Service Support Operations. Predictable unit movements and support operations can lead to increased vulnerability of both personnel (to include contracted support) and facilities. Unit commanders must understand that predictability places a higher demand on the unit's ability to know the local threat, assess unit vulnerabilities, and develop self-protection measures to include force-protection/anti-terrorism actions as they relate to the use of local national and TCN contractor support.

Summary and Observations

In this chapter we presented a five-step process for managing risk from Department of the Army (1998b) and Department of the Army et al. (2001) and introduced an approach to assessing causality, probability, and severity within that process. The process draws directly from Army and joint doctrine, and the approach draws from a combination of that doctrine and a technique known as fault tree analysis. We then applied the framework to a series of cost-related hazards that have been reported by GAO (2000a) report. We addressed other hazards through a more general risk-based lens. Consequently, we can identify lessons for the BSC, some of which may be applicable to other CSS contracts, to answer the questions posed at the outset of this report. Is the Army getting what it needs from its CSS contracts? Do those contracts present any unrecognized, unmitigated, or unnecessary risks? If the Army is not getting what it needs or is accepting inappropriate risks, what can it do about it? We present conclusions and lessons learned to address these questions in the following chapter.

However, to conclude this chapter, we bracket our comments by recalling that the BSC experience provides insight into many but not all of the risks relevant to CSS contracting, including some pertaining to performance and security. For example, the apparent readiness of the BSC in contrast to the reportedly slow initial implementation of LOGCAP in the Balkans suggests that the preparedness and flexibility embedded in—and observed in—an ongoing operation need not be present in a new venture. The pre-BSC Balkans contract experience provides evidence of performance risks that are not readily apparent in the BSC because the BSC is not really a new contract. Regarding security, reports of violence, injury, and death in other parts of world provide compelling reminders of the potential for physical harm. The Balkans may have proven to be a safer operating environment than others, or the Army's force-protection measures may have been better matched to the level of the threat.

CHAPTER FOUR

Conclusions and Lessons Learned

We began this report by asking three questions: Is the Army getting what it needs from its CSS contracts? Do those contracts present any unrecognized, unmitigated, or unnecessary risks? If the Army is not getting what it needs or is accepting inappropriate risks, what can it do about it? On the basis of the BSC, it would appear that the Army has been getting what it needs, though it may, at times, have accepted more cost risk than necessary to get it. Moreover, it may face additional risks relating to planning, coordination, and management because of the large number of contract participants, including government contracting and functional personnel drawn from several DoD agencies, various end users, and the contractor and its employees. In some instances, government contracting and functional personnel rotate through the theater on short tours and receive limited training on the administrative processes relevant to the BSC. Some end users also lack information about the contract and its particulars.

Nevertheless, the BSC appears to have performed as promised, insofar as its developers sought to implement a high-quality contract and, at least initially, to deemphasize cost. The GAO reports raise concerns about excess costs, most of which were modest and amenable to timely correction. Whether the Army accepted too much cost risk, particularly at the outset of the contract, remains an open question, given the totality of its objectives and the evolving nature of contract management. A customer may shift its focus to cost as a contract matures and conditions stabilize.

In considering readiness, the BSC appears to be a reliable and responsive arrangement, judging from its performance in the context of an ongoing operation. However, drawing a larger circle to include the pre-BSC contract activity under LOGCAP and other, more recent, contract activities in Afghanistan and Iraq, we see evidence of readiness-related risks in start-ups, deriving largely from more onerous planning, coordination, and management requirements.

In terms of higher-order concerns, the BSC also appears to be a relatively safe arrangement. However, also, on the basis of the larger circle, we see additional evidence of safety-related risk in less stable environments. In some, but not all, instances, the terms of a contract can address these risks.

To conclude, we draw together and highlight some of the key findings of this report to make the following three points:

- Not all risks are inherently contractual.
- A contract is only as good as its customer.
- Risk management is not risk elimination.

First, not all risks in the BSC are inherently contractual. The hypothetical illustrations and the discussion of the BSC track record suggest that relatively few risks arise directly—or only—from the decision to contract. Rather, most are inherent in particular activities or the operating environment. Choosing to use a contractor did precipitate some unique risks, such as those associated with the potential ambiguities of the status of contractor employees under the international law, the potential need for additional force protection in cases where contract employees are at risk of physical harm, the potential need for additional security restrictions when contractors hire foreign nationals, and clear differences in the chain of command. But either a contractor or an organic provider would have shouldered many other risks encountered in the Balkans, such as those induced by persistent changes in work scope and repeated loss of local experience as government contracting and functional personnel and end users rotated in and out. In fact, when observers point to frequent rotation as a source of difficulty overseeing the contract, they should also note that less frequent rotation of contractor employees brought marked benefits that an Army source, military or civilian, could not have provided under recent guidelines for temporary duty.

Second, a contract is only as good as its customer. The customer—and those acting on its behalf—must have the ability to plan, coordinate, and manage the contract. Performance will depend, in part, on how they undertake the source selection process and how they specify the terms of the contract. DoD contracting and functional personnel and end users must learn to coordinate their roles and, as applicable, employ management and oversight tools effectively. They must also understand their rights and responsibilities in relation to those of others. To the extent that planning, coordinating, managing, and using a performance-based contract—particularly one involving wide-ranging participation—requires special skills, DoD personnel and end users might require additional training to adequately perform these functions.

Speaking more generally, the call for coordination necessarily involves all participants, including the contractor and its employees. To integrate participants fully and promote cohesion, the customer must draw contractors into operational planning. It may also be necessary to recognize the role of the contractor in broader planning processes, which, although already occurring under the BSC and LOGCAP, may in other arenas present challenges to fundamental Army assumptions about the role of contractors. For example, at present, the doctrine behind the Total Army Analysis recognizes contractors and their employees as "augmenters," essentially providers of last resort. This implies an approach to evaluating and filling requirements fundamentally different from what would be needed if they were redefined as replacements. Nevertheless, the Army's use of contractors to provide CSS functions in the Balkans would seem to imply a role that goes beyond strict augmentation.

Effective management also requires visibility. Visibility facilitates planning and coordination—the TF commander must have a good idea how many people, including contract employees, will be physically present in the area of operations to accurately assess force protection and other support requirements, such as those for medical services. In short, the Army must know what its responsibilities are to the contractor and its employees, including whom it needs to protect.

Our third and final point reinforces Army doctrine on risk: that is, risk management is not risk elimination. This is often forgotten in discussions of how and when to use contractors. The commander obviously wants to anticipate hazards and reduce or avoid the risks associated with them when that is practical. But the commander also knows the value of maintaining flexibility to respond to unanticipated hazards. And the commander knows that, to achieve the Army's primary objectives in the theater, it may be necessary to accept some risks and their consequences. It may also be necessary to balance risk across competing objectives. This logic applies as well to effective application of contractors as it does to any other aspect of operational command.

Scope of Work and Work Breakdown Structure

The RFP, dated October 9, 1998, contains the following "scope of work," along with additional information—not presented here—on troop rotation, including expected duration and estimated number.[1]

The major functional areas include, but are not limited to, a full range of logistical support services, redeployment, demobilization, and periodic temporary construction for U.S. Forces and Multinational Stabilization Forces, as required. The contractor shall provide all resources and management to perform temporary base camp operations, planning and execution, and logistical services and prepare other designated support services for work, including a Life Support Area; Taszar Main, Hungary; a Staging and Materiel Support Area in Croatia; and the Area of Operations (AO) throughout Bosnia or any other location in the USAREUR area of responsibility necessary to support this effort. Continuous need for the services described may not exist. The government gives no assurance of a continuous need for these services or future requirements.

The RFP also includes requirements for "good commercial business standards" for the different WBSs. Table A.1 presents a sampling of the recurring services found in the RFP; as in the RFP, they are grouped by location and categorized into WBSs.[2]

---

[1] The words in this appendix were drawn largely from the RFP. However, some edits were made for consistency, clarity, and brevity.

[2] As noted in the RFP, "The recurring services listed below are grouped as they will be issued on the Task Orders (TO) listed in Section B and categorized into work breakdown structures," Section C, "Description/ Specifications/Work Statement," p. C-1, paragraph 3.

Table A.1
WBS in the Request for Proposal[a]

Hungary	Bosnia and Croatia
Base Camp Maintenance	**Base Camp Maintenance**
Provide base camp operations and maintenance, which includes repair and upkeep of equipment, facilities, streets, parking areas, and utilities	Provide daily collection, removal, and disposal of trash, food, septic, and medical waste
Provide bulk fuel delivery to power generators and heaters within the Taszar Support Base (TSB)	Operate and maintain power generation equipment at Bijeljina, Brcko, . . .
Provide potable water delivery for kitchens and shower facilities within the base camps	Provide vector control in all facilities and sites
Provide daily collection, removal, and disposal of trash, food, septic, and medical waste	Provide base camp operations and maintenance, which includes repair and upkeep of equipment, facilities, streets, parking areas, and utilities
Maintain power generation equipment at Taszar Airfield (TA), Taszar Main, and the Life Support Area	Provide work and service order response capabilities . . .
Operate and maintain utility supply and distribution systems	
Provide work and service order response capabilities . . .	
Laundry Service	**Laundry Operations**
Provide bundled laundry service (one 15-pound bundle per customer, twice weekly with no more that 72-hour turnaround time)	Provide bundled laundry service (one 15-pound bundle per customer, twice weekly with no more that 72-hour turnaround time)
Exchange, wash, and repair sleeping bags	Exchange and wash sleeping bags
Process medical laundry . . .	Process medical laundry . . .
Food Service Operations	**Food Service Operations**
Provide 24-hour food service operations (prepare three "A" ration meals per day utilizing government-furnished food and provide limited food service during nonmeal hours)	Provide 24-hour food service operations (prepare three "A" ration meals per day utilizing government-furnished food and provide limited food service during nonmeal hours)

Table A.1—continued

Hungary	Bosnia and Croatia
Supply Support Activity Operations	**Supply Service Activity Operations**
Provide aircraft refueling services at TA	Operate a supply support activity for U.S. military units only located at Guardian Base and Tuzla Main.
Operate a supply support activity at TA. Receive, store, issue, and account for Class II, III(P), IV, VII, and IX supplies for transiting forces and tenants	Receive, store, issue, and account for * Class II, III(P), IV, VII, and IX supplies
Operate the central issue point	**Class III Operations (Reordered)**
Provide direct support maintenance/ recovery services and backup organizational maintenance for deploying, redeploying, and tenant military units at the TSB	Operate and maintain Class III bulk storage yard for storage of 300,000 gallons JP8; 200,000 gallons diesel; 80,000 kerosene
Operate a supply support activity for U.S. military units only . . .	Operate and maintain Class III retail fuel points at Lukavac . . .
Equipment Maintenance	**Equipment Maintenance**
Maintain and operate a 24-point vehicle wash rack with high-pressure hoses 24 hours per day at debarkation points when required for troop rotation	Operate and maintain fully operational wash points at Base Camps Dobol, Demi, . . .
Operate a light/wheeled vehicle maintenance section for nontactical and tactical vehicles at the TSB	Operate a light/wheeled vehicle maintenance section for nontactical military equipment and for tactical vehicles in Slavonski Brod, Croatia
	Provide communication equipment maintenance for tactical communication systems in Slavonski Brod, Croatia. Maintenance personnel must have a secret security clearance and be U.S. citizens
Movements	**Movements**
Provide movement control team services for U.S. forces assigned, deploying, or redeploying throughout the AO	Provide air terminal movement control teams and/or Army departure/arrival control groups at Tuzla AB
Provide air terminal movement control teams and/or army departure/arrival control groups at TA . . .	As directed, operate military heavy equipment transporter trucks, palletized loading system vehicles, and tractor trailer rigs for onward movement missions from intermediate staging base Hungary to AO Bosnia and as directed
	Provide railhead operations at Lukavac

Table A.1—continued

Hungary	Bosnia and Croatia
Transportation	**Transportation**
Operate the trailer transfer point at TA	**Road Repairs and Maintenance**
Conduct transportation operations originating in Hungary and conducted throughout the AO and to and from the Central Region (CR)	Perform organizational maintenance support of the 38th engineer company (medium girder bridge) property at Slavonski Brod, Croatia
Operate local and line haul transportation of passengers and cargo	Provide snow and ice removal services in and around camps and troop occupied living/work/dining facilities
Provide and manage a marshaling area for the purpose of staging and processing vehicles and equipment for units deploying and redeploying through the TSB	Provide maintenance for roads and parking areas within base camps and access roads into and around base camps . . .
Provide railhead operations for deploying/redeploying units at the Taszar North and South Railheads . . .	
Management and Administration	**Management and Administration**
Container-Handling Services	**Container-Handling Services**
Operate and maintain a container handling yard at TA	Operate container yard at Comanche Base
Shuttle Bus Services	**Shuttle Bus Services**
Provide scheduled and on-call shuttle bus service between Taszar and Tuzla to support individual personnel replacements rotating in and out of the AO	Provide shuttle bus service as required in and around Tuzla Main to Tuzla West, Tuzla West Mayor Cell to Clam Shell . . .
Provide 24-hour shuttle bus services as required for U.S. forces, DoD civilian employees, and designated contractors in and around TSB	As required, maintain a 24-hour on-call shuttle bus capability to respond to unscheduled arrivals of troops, changes in troop flow requirements and intratheater shuttle bus services
Firefighting Services	**Mail Route Operations**
Provide continuous 24-hour, crash, rescue, and fire prevention and suppression services at the TSB	Provide bulk mail pickup and delivery (7 days a week) to and from the AO/central region. Pickup and delivery points are Frankfurt, Germany; Taszar Main, Hungary; and in Bosnia, Base Camps Demi, Dobol . . .
	Water Services
	Produce potable water for drinking, kitchens, and shower and medical facilities estimated at 25 gallons per soldier per day. Produce potable water for medical facilities estimated at 10,000 gallons per day

Table A.1—continued

Hungary	Bosnia and Croatia
Sale of Government Property	**Excess Property Laydown Yard and Scrap Metal Laydown Yard Operations and Management**
Sell surplus property as authorized by the plant clearance officer	Receive and store scrap to include packing/crating/handling for shipment. Provide sampling/analysis of HAZMAT and perform retrograde . . .
	Sell surplus property scrap and surplus serviceable or usable property per the direction of the plant clearance officer
Hazardous Waste Management	**Hazardous Waste Management**
Provide and maintain base camp accumulation points and hazardous waste areas for HAZMAT	Operate base camp accumulation points and hazardous waste storage areas (HWSAs). Assume HAZMAT generation of an estimated 500 liters per week per 500 troop population. Respond to minor (25 gallons or less) hazardous waste spills; accumulate and store hazardous waste at the HWSA. Transport all HAZMAT (solid, liquids, etc.) from the accumulation points to contractor operated HWSA
	Redeployment Staging Base Operations—Croatia
	Maintain and operate an estimated 50-point vehicle wash rack with high-pressure hoses 24 hours per day at debarkation points when required for troop rotation
	Support Services to the Multinational Stabilization Forces
	When authorized provide support services to non-U.S. members of the stabilization force

Table A.1—continued

Hungary	Bosnia and Croatia
Be Prepared for Missions	**Be Prepared for Missions**
Be prepared to conduct environmental/site restoration/dismantlement operations to restore government-utilized sites to original conditions	Be prepared to operate Class IV yards as required
Be prepared to provide services to assist in redeployment activities, which may include continuing or expanded performance of other missions. Activities may include vehicle fueling and defueling, 100% vehicle maintenance inspection, repair and/or maintenance services for onward-going vehicles . . .	Be prepared to establish and dismantle remote sites (temporary and/or permanent) on an as-directed basis
	Be prepared to dismantle and dispose of facilities and perform site restoration as governed by the lease or as directed by the ACO
Be prepared to operate a seaport reception staging and onward movement activity	Be prepared to conduct environmental/site restoration/dismantlement operations to restore government utilized sites to original condition
Be prepared to dismantle and dispose of facilities and perform site restoration as governed by the lease or as directed by the ACO	Be prepared to provide services to assist in redeployment activities, which may or may not include continuing or expanded performance of other missions. Activities may include vehicle fueling/defueling, 100% vehicle maintenance inspection, repair and/or maintenance services for onward-going vehicles . . .
Be prepared to provide retrograde	
Be prepared to provide temporary repair or construction services	
	Be prepared to support railhead operations at Brcko

[a]The home office would provide management and administration, mobilization and demobilization, freight, and insurance and benefits, including Defense Base Act Insurance under the WBS for the BSC.

Bibliography

BusinessWeek, International Edition, "Outsourcing War," September 15, 2003.

Department of Defense, Quadrennial Defense Review Report, September 30, 2001.

Department of the Army, *Contractor Deployment Gu*ide, PAM 715-16, February 27, 1998a.

_____, *Risk Management*, FM 100-14, Headquarters, Washington, D.C., April 23, 1998b.

_____, *Contractors Accompanying the Force*, AR 715-9, October 29, 1999.

_____, *Contractors on the Battlefield*, FM 3-100.21 (100-21), January 2003.

Department of the Army, Marine Corps, Navy, and Air Force, "Risk Management: Multiservice Tactics, Techniques, and Procedures," FM 3-100.12, MCRP 5-12.1c, NTTP 5-03.5, and AFTTP(I) 3-2.34, Air Land Sea Application Center, February 2001.

Filkins, Dexter, "U.S. Civilian Killed in Blast Near Tikrit," *New York Times*, August 6, 2003.

General Accounting Office (GAO), "Contingency Operations: Opportunities to Improve the Logistics Civil Augmentation Program," GAO/NSIAD-97-63, February 1997.

_____, "Contingency Operations: Army Should Do More to Control Cost in the Balkans," GAO/NSIAD-00-225, September 2000a.

_____, "Quality of Life for U.S. Soldiers Deployed in the Balkans," December 2000b.

_____, "Defense Budget, Contingency Operations in the Balkans May Need Less Funding in Fiscal Year 2003," GAO-02-1073, September 2002.

_____, "Contractors Provide Vital Services to Deployed Forces but Are Not Adequately Addressed in DOD Plans," GAO-03-695, June 2003.

Jones, Lt. Col. John R. "Thriving on Base Camps," *Engineer Professional Bulletin*, April 1997, downloaded reprint January 1, 2003, available at http://call.army.mil/products/trngqtr/tq4-98/jones.htm.

Kolar, Lt. Col. Nicholas, Jr., "LOGCAP: Providing Vital Services to Soldiers," *Engineer Professional Bulletin*, March 1997, available at http://call.army.mil/products/trngqtr/tq2-98/logcap.htm, accessed October 2001.

McElroy, Maj. Terry, "DLA in the Balkans," *Dimensions, the Defense Logistics Agency's News Magazine,* September/October 1999, available at http://www.dla.mil/Dimensions/Sept/Oct/DCMCBalkans.htm, accessed September 2002.

Merle, Renae, "More Civilians Accompanying U.S. Military," *Washington Post*, January 23, 2003, p. 10.

Risen, James, and Don Van Natta, Jr., "Plot to Poison Food of British Troops Is Suspected," *New York Times,* January 24, 2003, p. A1.

U.S. Army Corp of Engineers (USACE), "Logistics Civil Augmentation Program: A USACE Guide for Commanders," EP 500-1-7, December 5, 1994.

U.S. Army Corps of Engineers Transatlantic Programs Center (CETAC), Source Selection Plan, enclosure 2, 1997.

_____, Contract Announcement #98-16, "Utilities and Housekeeping Services: Broad-Spectrum Logistical Support Services for Deployed Forces in Hungary and the Balkans Region," August 20, 1998a.

_____, Solicitation No. DACA78-98-R-0028 for the Balkans Support Contract, October 1998b.

_____, "Augmenting the Military's Shortfalls: Overseas Contingency Operations," presented February 24, 1999a.

_____, "Standard Operating Procedures (SOP) for Task Orders on Balkans Support Contract (BSC)," November 23, 1999b.

_____, briefing, presented July 9, 2001a.

_____, "Contract Administrator's Most Frequently Asked Questions About the Balkans Support Contract, DACA78-99-D-0003, July 19, 2001b.

_____, "Award Fee Determining Plan for the Balkans Support Contract," September 2002a.

_____, "Users Guide for Writing a Performance-Based Services Statement of Work," 2002b.

_____, "Award Fee Evaluator Handbook for the Balkans Support Contract DACA78-99-D-0003," 2002c.

_____, briefing slides, presented May 2003.

_____, CETAC-OC, "Best Value Source Selection Guide to Best Practices," April 1997.

U.S. Army, Europe (USAREUR), "Base Camp Facilities Standards," also known as the "Red Book," March 25, 2002.

_____, "The USAREUR Blue Book: Base Camp Baseline Standards—A Guide to Base Operations Downrange," undated.

USAREUR and Seventh Army, "Contingency Operations Financial Management Implementation Instructions, FY 2002," 2001.

Wood, David, "Some of Army's Civilian Contractors Are No-Shows in Iraq," Newhouse News Service, available at http://www.newhouse.com, August 1, 2003.

Wood, Nicholas, "U.N. Officer Killed in Ambush in Kosovo," *Washington Post*, August 5, 2003, p. A9.

Wynn, Col. Donald T., "Managing the Logistics Support Contract in the Balkans Theater," Training Techniques, Fourth Quarter FY 2000, Center for Army Lessons Learned at http://call.army.mil/.